There are more than 300 verses i
even command, Christians to culti
are a genuine Christian (and are not backsliding), you know that growing in Christ is a very important, compelling, and alluring calling in your life. Paul Wells' *Growing in Christ* is a succinct, helpful, biblical, theological, and practical book on this subject that details enduring growth through five biblical steps: God's planting, being rooted, growing up, maturity, and fruitfulness. By the Spirit's grace, this book will instruct, edify, and mature you in our wonderful Savior, so that you will bear fruit to His glory.

Joel R. Beeke
President, Puritan Reformed Theological Seminary,
Grand Rapids, Michigan

Paul Wells writes with conviction and clarity, with care and compassion, with straightforward affection and a lively tone. He does not simply talk about spiritual growth and maturity, but urges us toward it—teaching, exhorting, and directing. This is not a shallow 'how to' manual, nor a heady discussion of spiritual development. It is a practical textbook for earnest Christians which combines insight with instruction, using the Word of God as a lamp to the feet and a light to the path. For those committed to growing more like Christ, or for those seeking to helping others grow, this will be a genuinely useful resource.

Jeremy Walker
Pastor, Maidenbower Baptist Church, Crawley, UK

I've seen grace and knowledge embodied in Paul Wells, the two essential aspects of spiritual growth. I hope many find not only help in this book, but also experience growth in Christ.

Jose de Segovia
Teacher, journalist & theologian, Madrid, Spain

Authored by a lifelong defender of biblical truth, this book provides a healthy corrective for any who imagine that spiritual growth can bypass robust theology.

James Hely Hutchinson
Director, Institut Biblique de Bruxelles

Growing in Christ is a biblical and theological feast that encourages readers to hunger for more. Regardless of where you may be on your Christian journey, this personal, practical and enjoyable guide offers rich nourishment for the soul. I will return often to Paul Wells' simple but profound study on Christian growth.

Peter A. Lillback
President, Westminster Theological Seminary, Philadelphia, Pennsylvania

Reading this book is to benefit from Paul Wells' own deep rootedness in the Scriptures. Here is a strong biblical call to Christian growth, shaped by the Bible's vivid pictures – from being planted in good soil all the way to bearing much good fruit. In a world calling us to question any truth outside ourselves, we need this urgent and encouraging reminder of our true calling to grow in the grace and knowledge of the Lord Jesus.

Kathleen Nielson
Author, speaker

Even in church circles, our culture is marked by a pragmatic mindset and looks for easy-steps towards progress, Christian discipleship is at risk of becoming a technique to be grasped or a program to deliver. Paul Wells convincingly argues that our growth in Christ needs to be pursued according to God's criteria as they are revealed in His Word. What a feast it is to be accompanied by a seasoned theologian to delve into the biblical path leading to Christian maturity. This is a 'calvinian' book where reformed theology matches its biblical richness with pastoral warmth and practical encouragements.

Leonardo De Chirico

Pastor of the church Breccia di Roma
Lecturer in Historical theology at Istituto di Formazione Evangelica e Documentazione (Padova, Italy) and director of the Refomanda Iniatiative

Growing in Christ

5 Biblical Steps for Enduring Growth

Paul Wells

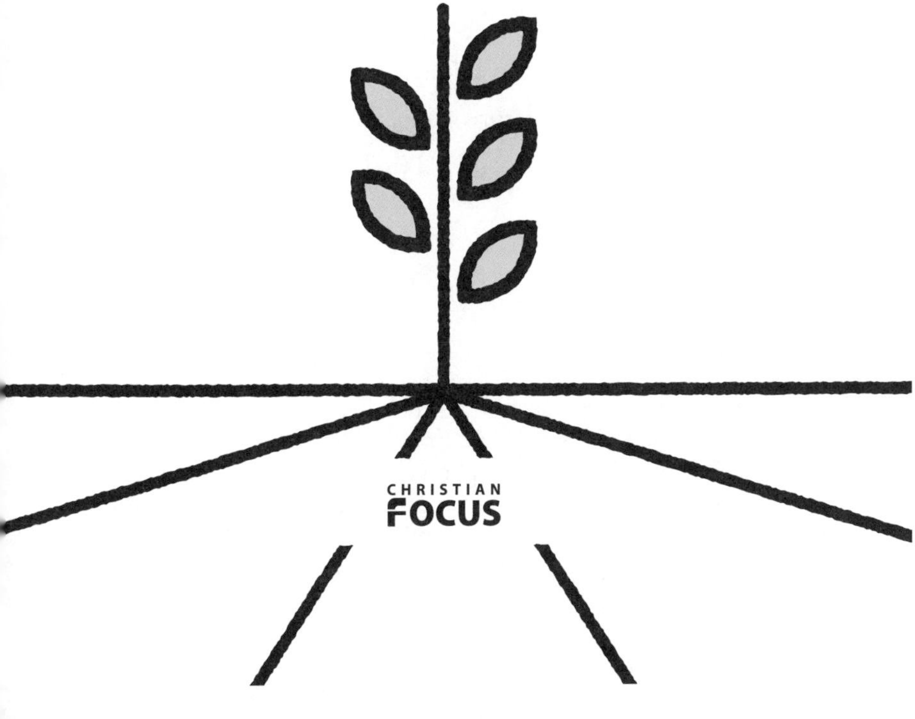

CHRISTIAN
FOCUS

Unless otherwise stated, Scripture quotations are from the *Holy Bible, English Standard Version*, ESV® Text Edition: 2016. Copyright © 2001 by Crossway Bibles, a publishing ministry of Good News Publishers.

Some Scripture quotations are the author's own paraphrase.

Other Christian Focus Publications titles by Paul Wells:
Cross Words: The Biblical Doctrine of the Atonement (2006)
Taking the Bible at its Word (2013)

Paperback ISBN 978-1-5271-0893-6
Ebook ISBN 978-1-5271-0982-7

10 9 8 7 6 5 4 3 2 1

Published in 2022
by
Christian Focus Publications Ltd,
Geanies House, Fearn, Ross-shire,
IV20 1TW, United Kingdom.

www.christianfocus.com

Cover design by Pete Barnsley

Printed and bound by
Bell & Bain, Glasgow

MIX
Paper from
responsible sources
FSC® C007785

CONTENTS

Introduction: Why Is Christian Growth Important?............9

1. God's Planting..........23

2. Being Rooted..........49

3. Growing Up..........79

4. Maturity..........111

5. Fruitfulness..........139

Conclusion..........169

Appendix..........177

INTRODUCTION

Why Is Christian Growth Important?

Growth in Christ, what we can expect
Knowledge of God's grace is central
Biblical images for growth
Conditions for growth
Summary, and the way ahead

Introduction theme: *A key theme in the Bible is that God's presence transforms deserts into gardens. What is true of the big project for the world and His people is also true for individual lives. Faith in Christ grows and bears fruit, resisting adverse pressures in a hostile world. Flourishing in the wasteland is achieved by 'growing in the* grace and knowledge *of our Lord and Saviour Jesus Christ'. Followers of Christ grow because they know* who *they believe,* what *they believe and* why *they believe it. The Bible illustrates these foundational realities and uses key images for growth. It also indicates the conditions that favour it, and the successive stages of growing up into Christ.*

There are lots of books on Christian growth, many of them very good. However, if you randomly pick one out the chances are you'll get a sort of Christian self-help manual, majoring in 'how it feels' to be a believer, rather than a biblical approach. Therefore, this book is a biblical presentation of how we should approach growth into Christ.

Have you noticed any changes in the attitudes of Christians in recent years? It could well be the case. Many things that used to be thought of as bad or wrong are accepted by those around us. The juggernaut of social progress is gathering speed on the highway to change and believers are dragged along in the slipstream. Traditional attitudes are left behind and the new normals become commonplace. The passing of former moral values influenced by Christianity is now almost complete and we are into a time when new values are being normalised.

We would be wrong to think this doesn't influence the life of the average believer or what is acceptable in church communities. Pressures to conform are becoming more compelling. Christians must either get on board without question or have a good reason for resisting.

A current idea is that if faith is going to survive in the post-truth world, a new more relaxed approach centred on personal feelings and expectations must be adopted.

Winners and losers

This is not to say that the past was necessarily better and the present is always worse, but at least we should be aware of what's happening. One of the big losers in the ballpark of upbeat believing is *the content* of faith. Ultimately this impacts everything else, but are we really convinced of its importance? What used to be called teaching, doctrine, theology, or any form of reflection is sidelined as 'head knowledge'. Group Bible studies are often free-for-all discussions, sometimes the pooling of ignorance. Those who want something deeper can follow online courses or go to seminars. Teaching and discipling are low on the radar of the average church programme; being friendly and relevant is pretty high. What is all important is not primarily what God says in Scripture, but how we feel about ourselves.

This devaluation of content is surprising. Apart from the fact that what Christians think and believe and not what they feel makes them different from those around, our age has seen an explosion of information technology. 'The science' is the be-and end-all of decision making. Knowledge is at a premium in educational systems and professional training. Parents want the best for their kids and measure growth by ticking the boxes of progress reports. Knowledge is important for jumping through the hoops on the path to success.

So what are the expectations for knowledge and growth in normal Christian living? How do we value them? Is it so important as to be considered something worth striving for, or is it simply an elitist luxury? So what, if it is an optional extra? Many Christians, including those who are well up the professional ladder, seem happy to muddle through life's challenges with a lowest common denominator understanding of faith. This is surprising and no wonder if they express that something is missing from their way of being Christians.

Measuring growth

This attitude leads to a worrying question for many believers, particularly after a few years of Christian involvement. It can become acute if mid-life crises arise, when the doldrums of routine, imperceptible progress, or disappointment take the wind out of our sails. Am I growing at all as a Christian? How can I measure it, and is there any way of measuring?

There is no one simple answer to those questions for everyone, nor any pat answers, because we are all different. Many factors are involved because as believers we are all at different stages in growth, and we have all begun with different personal life experiences. However, three comments are relevant.

Firstly, many Christians have never thought seriously about what growth is, or even whether it is important. It's taken for granted, perhaps with only a minimal awareness of the biblical markers that will be presented in the following chapters.

Secondly, growth is naturally rather rapid at the beginning of the Christian life, full of discoveries and new insights. The changes are obvious to us and to those around. Later things plateau out, and progress is less evident. I see my grandchildren in the USA once a year. How fast they grow up! But they do not see much change in me, all they see is an ageing dude!

Finally, and because of this, growth is measured in terms of lifetimes, not weeks or months. We can look back over our journey of life and think of how problems that were enormous back then are manageable now. Or we can think of how we handled a crisis in the past, where we went wrong, and how we have learned something from it. More concretely, we can look at the faults, often secret and unknown to others, that have been overcome because we have learnt, with the Lord's help, to deal with them.

When we take stock in this way it's not with a view to patting ourselves on the back. While being thankful for spiritual growth, we should also be humbled because we recognise God's grace has been imperceptibly at work. Moreover, we still struggle with our imperfections and are far from the goal. What was true for the apostle Paul, as he expressed it in Philippians 3:12, is much more so of us: 'Not that I… am already perfect, but I press on to make it my own, because Christ Jesus has made me his own.'

What we must avoid is a defeatist mindset from the get-go. The temptation is to say: 'there's nothing that can be done there, because that's me, I'm just like that.' If that's our attitude, we'll starve ourselves of the means of growth. The end product will be discouragement and indifference, leading to spiritual depression.

Grace and knowledge

The focus of this book is specifically on growing in Christ, leaving aside the broader issues of church life and its importance for sanctification, or the practice of prayer. The question of how to grow and be stable in Christ is one of the most important ones we face, either for the present or the future life.

Biblically speaking, the two essential ingredients in spiritual growth are grace and knowledge, not feelings, self-image, ministries or programmes. Grace and knowledge are siamese twins, birthed by understanding of Scripture as God's revealed Word, and the Spirit of God. One never goes without the other. God's grace brings a corresponding deepening of knowledge, which in turn stimulates the desire to know more of the wonders of grace. Knowledge is not knowing things *about* God, but a deeper personal appreciation of God Himself: His wonder, the greatness and the glory of His ways and works. The Psalms repeatedly refer to the 'steadfast love of God' in action, which leads to praise for who God is.[1]

The beginning of the four Gospels in the New Testament present the fulcrum of God's plan of salvation. In John's Gospel in particular the arrival of the Lord Jesus on the world scene sets the tone for the grace-knowledge relationship. He

1. Psalms 36:7-10, 89:1-2, 14.

personally embodies them both. God's incarnate Son dwelt 'among us full of grace and truth'. The apostle Peter, one of the eyewitnesses who also heard the Father's words on the mount of transfiguration, exhorts believers to 'growth in the grace and knowledge of our Lord and Saviour Jesus Christ'.[2] Knowledge of God and recognition of His grace and truth is the way to growth and stability. Maturity is the opposite of being blown about by every 'wind of doctrine'.[3] Christians are not the barometers of the present climate; they have a thermostat set by God's revealed Word.

Isn't it a tragedy when children don't grow as expected? A comparable tragedy is when people who have been Christians for a good while are indifferent, or show no sign of growth. Is it because grace and knowledge have had little impact on their lives that many buckle when they run into the first real test? Or when they lack consistency by following the latest religious fads, or when they are unaware that the world's agenda is moulding their views?

The danger is that unwittingly, people who take themselves to be Christians may really be dead on the vine, not producing any fruit by growth into Christ. The grace and knowledge duo has not had any real or practical impact. It's tragic that folks go through life clocking up sermon hours week in week out, with little sign of change. Eventually its absence leads someone to question the reality of faith and its practical usefulness. People become lukewarm and indifferent, or church hoppers. Perhaps they eventually quit altogether.

Even a superficial reading of the New Testament shows how vital the notion of growth is. One of Jesus' iconic parables, known as 'the Sower', about how seed grows, sets the tone. The story is about the spiritual reality of God's kingdom and the

2. John 1:14, 2 Peter 3:18.

3. John 1:14, 17, 2 Peter 1:18, 3:18, Ephesians 4:14.

way it comes into the world. From the insignificant beginning of a seed falling in the ground, much fruit is produced. The unexpected miracle of Christ's kingdom is that it goes from almost nothing to astonishing outcomes.

That is what we can legitimately expect as well.

Biblical images of growth

The farming culture of biblical times provided a rich backdrop for suggestive teaching about spiritual growth. Vines, olives and fig trees were used as symbols for Israel as God's people.

Several biblical images about personal growth refer to sowing, favourable places for planting, trees blossoming and producing fruit. By way of contrast, unfavourable conditions lead to negative equity in growth. The prophet Jeremiah was not a crowd-pleaser. The unbelievers of Judea had turned away from God, trusting for help from alliances with the superpowers. They were like 'a shrub in the desert, and shall not see any good come … dwelling in the parched places of the wilderness in an uninhabited salt land'.[4]

Jesus chose a crucial moment, just before His death, to teach His disciples about 'abiding in him' as 'the true vine' in order to 'bear much fruit'. He added:

> If you abide in me and my words abide in you, ask whatever you wish, and it will be done for you. By this is my Father glorified, that you bear much fruit and so prove to be my disciples.[5]

This is rather remarkable. Believers show themselves to be true disciples by asking God 'whatever they wish' *in order to bear*

---

4. Jeremiah 17:5-6. Cf. Ezekiel 17:1-10.
5. John 15:7-8.

fruit. This is the result of the life-giving presence and power of Jesus' words. The Father is glorified when His Son's Word abides in us and as a result we trust in Him. Everything we desire is received from Him by doing this. What should we ask for? Not random things like a new car or a holiday abroad, but for growth in Christ through His Word, blossoming into the assurance that we are true disciples.

Several times in the New Testament we come across another illustration. Children grow to maturity when they move from a diet of milk to solid food.[6] In 1 Corinthians 13:8-12, the apostle Paul underlined the centrality of love in the pilgrimage of believers from time to eternity. He chose an illustration contrasting what children and adults know to describe the continuity and the difference between the present and the future. Both of them know the same reality, but adults have deeper perception than kids. A child knows their parent goes to work every day, but has very little idea of what they actually do there. The Christian life is all about living well and enjoying life in Christ now, and subsequently growing up to adulthood in eternity.

Living as we do in an age of 'how to' books it strikes us as surprising that there is no 'self-help' letter on Christian growth in the New Testament. Why don't we find something like John Calvin's 'golden book of the Christian life' in his *Institutes* (III:6-10)? There are many reasons, but perhaps the main one is that the New Testament is not primarily about our needs, or our performance, but about what God has graciously done for us, and His glory. As we see our lives associated with God's story of grace we find ourselves as believers, and at the same time we find what we can aim for. 'This is your life' becomes meaningful when we see our story in the light of the story of

---

6. 1 Corinthians 3:2, 1 Peter 2:2-3, Hebrews 5:12-13.

Christ: His life, death, resurrection, ascension, reign and return in glory to bring in the new creation.

At a certain moment the penny drops. Christ is my destiny, and all my life from beginning to end is wrapped up in Him, who He is and what He did.[7] Christian growth is all about living in Christ and growing into Him, day by day, year after year, until He says, 'Well done, it's time to come on up here with me'.

Conditions for growth

In the natural realm, growth is something of a mystery. Two plants stand side by side, one does well and the other doesn't grow.

Think of the adjacent houses Jesus pictured in the parable at the end of the Sermon on the Mount. Both looked the same, appeared to be solidly built, at least until a weather bomb demolished one of them. The reason for this was a hidden fault, namely the lack of a sure foundation. Sand provides no stability.[8]

So spiritual growth is not something to turn into a method, a twelve-step programme, with results guaranteed. Thinking about growing, analysing it, and seminars might help, but they do not automatically promote personal growth. It is something that happens naturally in Christ, when the conditions are right. Spiritual vitality is a living and personal walk with Christ. As any gardener knows, growth requires loving care and cultivation in the right conditions.

How then can the conditions of spiritual growth be described? A comparison may help. Photosynthesis is a chemical

---

7. Cf. Ephesians 1:4-15. Note the repeated references to 'in him' in this text.

8. Matthew 7:24-27.

reaction in plants you probably heard about at school. Light, carbon dioxide and water are the conditions necessary for life and growth. Carbon dioxide enters through the underside of leaves, water through roots, and in sunlight the plant releases oxygen into the air and makes glucose for growth.

Light, water and air are vital to plant growth. Put a plant in the dark, or water too much, and you'll kill it. So also there are important factors for growth in the spiritual sphere. The right conditions are necessary for life to flourish in Christ.

Several factors are included in the biblical conditions for life and growth. The context must be right, with rooting in good soil and exposure to light. Growth is maturing in strength. Finally the fruit appears. This way of seeing spiritual growth is useful, because it is biblical. Psalm 92:12-15 describes it in a few brush strokes, with the key words in italics (added):

> The righteous *flourish* like the palm tree
> and *grow* like a cedar in Lebanon.
> They are *planted* in the house of the LORD;
> they *flourish* in the courts of our God.
> They still *bear fruit* in old age:
> they are ever *full of sap* and green,
> to declare the LORD is upright:
> he is my rock and there is no unrighteousness in him.[9]

Here we get down to basics. The growth process is described by five factors that provide the right conditions: planting, flourishing, growing, being full of vitality, and fruitfulness. Together these apply to the Christian life and how it is lived throughout our earthly journey.

Paul takes up the psalmist's image in a collective way when he writes to believers at pagan Corinth. In 1 Corinthians he

---

9. See also Psalm 1:3, Jeremiah 17:5-10, Ezekiel 19:10-14, 47:12, Revelation 22:14.

reprimands them because of their factions, reminding them that Paul, Apollos or Peter are only servants each with a part to play:

> I planted, Apollos watered, but God gave the growth. So neither he who plants nor he who waters is anything, but only God who gives the growth. He who plants and he who waters are one, and each will receive his wages according to his labour. For we are God's fellow workers. You are God's field, God's building.[10]

Paul uses mixed metaphors of the field, the building and the workers to describe a construction that grows harmoniously according to God's design.

What applies to individuals applies also to faithful churches. Nothing could remind us more clearly that when individuals are growing up into Christ, the believing community also grows. When a living church grows, believers who are part of it also grow. Little room is left for praise of leaders, who are simply servants. 'Only God gives the growth'. It's not bad to remember that in a day of megachurches and superstar internet preachers.

Summary, and the way ahead

Sad to say, one reason life today is a challenge for many believers is because of the wishy-washy teaching in the churches. There may well be sleeping Christians in gospel churches where the leaders preach their hearts out. They need to wake up and get real about their laid-back attitudes. The context is right but they are indifferent and static. There may also be young, stalled believers with a desire to grow in half-dead churches. These places have the name but not the nature of a true church, because their teaching is indifferent to biblical truth. If believers

10. 1 Corinthians 3:6-9.

stick around there long, they will not grow and eventually the lack of light, water or the poor soil will stunt them. The biblical ideal for health and holiness is the growing Christian in a living church.

In the following chapters the biblical factors for conditions favourable to growth into Christ will be presented in this order:

1. *Planting* in the right place for spiritual life to begin

2. *Rooting* in the biblical teaching of the Word of God

3. *Growing up* to stability in Christ

4. *Maturity and vitality* through the work of the Spirit

5. *Fruitfulness* as the outcome of growth into Christ.

The growth process is dynamic. We will describe how, as believers, we can benefit in a practical way from the conditions for growth in Christ. It's also exciting, like graduating from primary to secondary school, moving from the second to the first team, or getting that first job. The different stages are mileposts on the path of progress.

Finally, it's wonderful because growth is growth in God's grace. We should never cease to be amazed by what God has done for us and is doing in us and in others on the way with us.

QUESTIONS FOR DISCUSSION

1. What are the main problems preventing spiritual growth today?
2. Why is spiritual growth important?
3. What is the link between grace and knowledge?
4. Discuss the biblical images for growth.
5. Why is the right context for growth important?

6. Can you name the biblical conditions for growth in Christ?
7. Can you evaluate your growth in Christ?
8. Are you in the right place to encourage growth in Christ in your own life?

1

GOD'S PLANTING

Beginnings
Growth is about God's kingdom
Exodus, vines and olives
Our place in God's growth plan
Word and Spirit in beginnings
A question of life and death

Chapter theme: *God's act of planting is the beginning of growth. God is the giver of life, and spiritual life begins with Him. The biblical pattern for beginnings is presented by God's acts in creation, in the exodus from Egypt, and in the coming of God's kingdom in Jesus Christ. Personal growth which begins with regeneration and new birth is an aspect of God's planting of His people. It is part of God's new creation, accomplished by His Word and Spirit. It plants new life in a world that is passing away.*

Beginnings are important because they are a taste of what lies ahead. Sometimes they are frightening because of the unknown factor. Remember the first day at a new school, a new job, or that first date with your soulmate?

The two parables referred to in the introduction namely the sower and the seed and the two houses, show the importance of beginnings.[1] It may not be immediately evident, but they are crucial.

In the first story about the way seed grows, the determining factor is where it falls to begin with. If it's on the path, the stony ground, or among weeds, it may do well for a time, then the inevitable decline sets in. In the parable of the two houses, what matters is not how the two are photo-brushed, but the fact that one has good foundations and the other hasn't. One crashes down in the storm because the builder hadn't bothered to dig down to the rock. What Jesus was saying is this: not getting rid of sin through serious repentance is like not removing the landfill in order to make a building solid. That sort of life won't stand up to adversity. The moral of the story in both cases is the warning, 'Don't take appearances for reality'. Things might seem right, but what is essential is the hidden beginning—where the seed is planted and where the building sits firmly. All our projects, and life itself, must begin God's way.

Psalm 107 begins the fifth book of the Psalter with a song about how God is found by people in dire situations. It concludes, 'Whoever is wise, let him attend to these things; let them consider the steadfast love of the Lord.' Fruitfulness in the life of God's people begins with 'his wondrous works to the children of men'. Verses 33-38 state what the Lord does to change lives:

1. Matthew 13:1-9, 16-23; 7:24-27.

> He (the Lord) turns rivers into a desert,
> springs of water into thirsty ground,
> a fruitful land into a salty waste,
> because of the evil of its inhabitants.
> He turns a desert into pools of water,
> a parched land into springs of water.
> And there he lets the hungry dwell
> and they establish a city to live in;
> they sow fields and plant vineyards,
> and get a fruitful yield.
> By his blessing they multiply greatly…

In this chapter we'll think about the importance of beginning right for subsequent Christian growth.

Begin at the beginning

Love and wonder were in the air when God began His new production, and it was 'very good'. The Bible opens with seven momentous words in Hebrew: 'In the beginning God created the heavens and the earth'. Before that there was nothing but the personal eternal Trinity: Father, Son and Spirit. The first verse in Genesis 1 sums up the loving work of creation. God acted from nothing, with nothing, into nothing. That's impossible to understand! The outcome was a universe with space, time and living creatures.

Einstein once wrote in a letter, 'God does not play dice with the universe'.[2] That's true in biblical terms as well. An almighty all-wise God is not a chancer. Creation established His *kingdom,* His place of rule. Creatures had their place and their function because the creator separated them from one another with His structuring commands. It was a healthy, holy and happy place.

2. Responding to another physicist in 1926.

A song to God's glory rang round the globe from every living creature.

Creation was not the utopian 'garden of delights' visionaries dream about. In the beginning it was a place where God was worshipped by His creatures living the way He intended. Creaturely callings that reflect God's great love and freedom were gifts to His kingdom servants. Man gave names to the animals as God's shop steward. The beginning included the mutual recognition of man and woman as partners. With the help of God's grace human beings would discover the meaning of harmonious living without waste or exploitation. So the kingdom of love and justice would come, for God's glory and creation's good.

Scripture also tells us about a second new beginning, even more momentous and breathtaking than the first. It includes two perspectives—the final renewal of all things in the new creation reign of Jesus after His return, and the 'washing of regeneration and renewal of the Holy Spirit', the new birth of personal salvation.[3] When the kingdom of God is established in glory the new universe will emerge from the disappearance of the old world of sin, sorrow and death. It will be the final, renewed, spiritual world that we call a 'heavenly' reality, over which God will reign as Lord of all.

Creation mark 2 is planted here and now in the old world in God's kingdom of grace. Every day it grows, until Christ comes again in glory. Personal salvation through faith in Christ is not something separate from this cosmic process. It belongs to it. Our being planted and growing in Christ is not just some individual experience, but an integral part of God's plan for His universe. The temptation for us is to concentrate on the individual dimension and forget the big picture. When we see that our renewal is included in a cosmic dimension, it's all the

3. Matthew 19:28, Titus 3:5. In Greek *palingenesia*, 'creation again'.

more astonishing. Human life begins at conception and our part in the new creation is like that of a cell in the foetus. We grow together with all the other cells until the new creation is born.

The coming of Jesus into this world is the seed that plants the new kingdom of God. From this God's new eternal kingdom develops and grows. That's why it's important to understand beginnings.

Creation Mark 2

The second beginning of creation is not a straight line from the first. New hope is injected decisively into a situation of brokenness and despair. Social progress is a hope for many people, but you have to be blind not to see that the world is evil and unjust. Isn't that why we want progress? As G.K. Chesterton famously remarked, 'Original sin is the one point of Christian theology that easily can be proved empirically.'[4] Transgression, disobedience and death brought mayhem into God's good world. God was the author of an orderly creation; man countered it by an act of anti- or de-creation. Once the bell of revolt had tolled, there was no un-ringing it. Nor did the chime fade away. It gets louder throughout history. Rebellion becomes more and more firmly rooted in systemic injustice, empowering empires of evil. The book of Daniel describes them as being like an imposing statue, albeit with weak feet of mixed iron and clay. It looks impressive but the hybrid foundation is its Achilles' heel. A rolling stone, not cut by human hands, a prophetic picture of Jesus' coming kingdom, brings it down. The kingdom of God, unlike human empires, will never be destroyed.[5] How imposing the Soviet imperium looked until 1989 when it came tumbling down!

4. G.K. Chesterton, *Orthodoxy,* 1908, chap. 2.

5. Daniel 2:44-45, Revelation 11:15.

The dramatic coming of God's kingdom is seen in the abrupt start to Mark's Gospel: 'Beginning of the gospel of Jesus Christ, the Son of God… Jesus came into Galilee, proclaiming the good news of God and saying, The time is fulfilled and the kingdom of God is at hand; repent and believe the gospel.'[6] Mark's opening salvo is the word 'beginning' (*archē*), echoing the first word of Genesis (*bĕrei'shit*). When Jesus takes the stage God's good news intercepts lives of emptiness, deserts without form and void.[7]

John the Evangelist wrote his Gospel later than Mark. He took up the lead about the beginning, but gave it a different spin. 'In the beginning was the Word, and the Word was with God, and the Word was God. He was in the beginning with God.'[8] Note that John does not say 'and God was the Word'. If he'd done so he would have denied the personal distinction between God the Father and God the Son. That distinction is eternally real. It means that the Son has personal and eternal existence in His divine nature alongside the Father. It also accounts for the coming of Jesus, introduced later in verse 14: 'And the Word became flesh and dwelt among us, and we have seen his glory, the glory of the only begotten of the Father full of grace and truth' (NIV). The wonder is that the Son, who is eternal with the Father *before* the beginning, became human flesh in a fallen world. His two distinct natures were joined seamlessly in one person.

This is a radical new beginning. There's nothing comparable to it in the world's religions. Jesus' incarnation plants God's second creation! In the new beginning Jesus brought life and light, and began to do away with the old. He drank the dregs of human brokenness by taking human sin and God's rejection upon Himself. He died because of them, putting them to death

6. Mark 1:1, 14-15.

7. Mark 1:1-2, 14-15. Cf. Genesis 1:1-2.

8. John 1:1-2.

in His body. Out of seeming defeat came victory and new life from death. By His resurrection Jesus ushered in the cosmic dimension of the new creation that began with Him the first Christmas Day.

Resurrection from death to newness of life, the injection of the new into the old, is the prime focus of Christian life. In 2 Corinthians 5:17 Paul boldly states, 'Anyone in Christ is a new creation, the old things are passed away, all things have become new.' Rebirth is more than just a change we undergo, real as it may be. It's God's planting us into Christ's new creation kingdom, and into Christ Himself. Nothing is ever the same again. Life is recreated. The promise of the kingdom is return from exile to order and kingdom happiness. That's why the good news about Jesus majors in 're-' words: recreation, rebirth, redemption, reconciliation, and renewal.[9] All of them mean a new beginning, a second chance for creation.

Towards the end of his life John put this idea in an even bigger frame in his book of Revelation. With a glimpse backward to the prophet Isaiah, John said several times that Jesus is the beginning and the end of everything.[10] Jesus is 'the first and the last', the beginning, the centre and finality, the Lord of all creation.[11] The Lordship of Christ over everything is the last word about it, guaranteed by the resurrection from the dead. This is why Jesus told His disciples on taking leave of them in Matthew 28:20, 'All authority in heaven and on earth has been given to me… I am with you always to the end of the age.' Jesus' authority is His power over all things from

9. See Paul Wells, *Cross Words: The Biblical Doctrine of the Atonement*, (Christian Focus, 2006), ch. 15.

10. 'Alpha and omega' are the first and last letters of the Greek alphabet.

11. Revelation 1:8, 21:5-8, 22:12-15. The Old Testament rabbis used this expression in Hebrew, see Isaiah 44:6 and 48:12. In the Hebrew alphabet the first, middle and last letters (aleph, mem and tav) make the word *emet* (אמת) meaning truth.

the beginning to the end of creation. After the resurrection His kingship is declared publicly in His power over sin, death, hell and the devil.

When we become new creatures in Christ by faith we find that we are one minute bit of the trillion-piece cosmic jigsaw that makes up God's plan, overseen by the person and work of Jesus. Nothing could change a same old, same old life more than that! We may just be little pieces in a big picture, but without us it is incomplete. Little but important in God's plan is our destiny. That's why this world will not end until the last believer to be saved is safe in Christ's kingdom.

The second chance God

Who wouldn't like to rip a few pages out of their past life and start afresh? Back in the bad old days of school ink-wells and pens that always blotted exercise books, I would try to get away with mistakes by ripping a page out. The more I did it, the more obvious it was, because the book became thinner. Changing the past is impossible, because we have become what we have been, and it can never be eradicated. With the internet it's even worse; our mistakes follow us like slugs' tracks on the path. What wouldn't we give to cut free and begin again!

God planted a garden, but the revolution of sin planted thorns and thistles that can't be uprooted. Sin is a form of slavery. In another of Jesus' parables, thorns and thistles grow together with good seed until the final harvest.[12]

The reason sin ends up in slavery is that it subjects human beings to false gods or idols. If we are not what we eat and we do not always merit the leaders we have, we certainly do become like the idols we worship. We are blind, deaf, and dumb to the creator who made us. God's acts of salvation that

12. The parable of the good seed and the weeds, Matthew 13:24-30, 36-43.

deliver from bondage are always acts of judgment against sin. That's the message of Scripture focussed on the grace of the cross where Jesus suffered judgment for our sin. God does not hate His creatures; it's our sin that is hateful and we don't like to admit it.

God is the great abolitionist who liberates by freeing sinners from slavery. His kingdom comes when He brings freedom by turning the tables on our idols. The biblical history of salvation is one of God sending freedom fighters to free His people. He redeems them, or buys them back, from sin.

Freedom in the Old Testament invariably follows the model of the exodus from Egypt under Moses and Aaron. Life in Egypt for the children of Abraham was no cruise on the Nile; it was hard labor and oppression, with vicious slave drivers. Making bricks without straw to the glory of Pharaoh and his pagan idolatry of death was the routine of captivity. In the end even Jewish babies were killed off. The people groaned for release. Egypt was 'the house of bondage', a symbol of sin itself. God intervened in a miraculous way and saved His people from sin's power. He called them to Sinai, gave them a law of liberty, then led them to the land promised to Abraham, where they were to put it into practice. God planted His people in Palestine to be a 'holy nation', different from any other. This was the first step of God's plan for the restoration of a fallen world.

Vines and olives

Palestine was to be a land 'flowing with milk and honey', a new garden of Eden with God ruling over His people. The Israelites were often disobedient children, and tried the Lord's patience sorely, but the sacrificial system provided atonement from sin and renewed fellowship with God. Freed from the slavery of Egypt, God planted His people in the promised land to grow and flourish as a light to the nations. The vine and the olive tree, both common sights in Palestine, were symbols of Israel's calling.

Psalm 80:8-9 describes the destiny of unfaithful Israel and the hope for the coming of a 'son of man' to restore it: 'You brought a vine out of Egypt; you drove out the nations and planted it. You cleared the ground for it; it took deep root and filled the land.' Hosea 10:1 calls Israel 'a luxuriant vine that yields its fruit'. But it came to yield bitter grapes. The choice vine became wild and degenerate, useful only as fuel for the fire.[13] When Jesus said, 'I am the true vine, and my Father is the vinedresser', His disciples really got what He was talking about. He was claiming to be none other than God's true Israel.

The olive tree was also an important symbol of God planting Israel to worship and serve Him. In the Temple, following the instructions given to Moses on Sinai, stood the Menorah, the seven-branched candlestick, which is incidentally the emblem of modern-day Israel. God said to Moses in Exodus 25:31-32 (NIV):

> Make a lampstand of pure gold… its flowerlike cups, buds and blossoms shall be of one piece with it. Six branches are to extend from the sides of the lampstand—three on one side and three on the other.

Some interpretations propose that the six branches represent the days of creation, with the seventh day of rest in the centre. We know what it looked like because it is pictured on the Arch of Titus in Rome with troops carrying it off when the Temple was destroyed in 70 A.D. Israel was planted like a flourishing

13. Isaiah 5:1-2, Jeremiah 2:21, Ezekiel 15:6. Jesus made the vineyard a symbol for Israel and God's judgment in Mark 12:1-12. Thorns are a symbol of sin and unfruitfulness. See Matthew 7:16 and Isaiah 5:6.

olive tree with oil lighting the branches.[14] As God's creation, His chosen people were to bring the light of God's kingdom to the nations and to model the true sense of worship and service in a world of slavery and false gods. Paul's use of the olive tree imagery for Israel in Romans 11:17-24 tells how God saves all His people.

In the Old Testament the emphasis is on God's adoption of Israel as His people and the call for collective fruitfulness in witness to the world. However, the individual aspect is not absent. The righteous person is presented in the first Psalm as a tree planted by the water, bearing fruit in season, in contrast with the wicked who are like husks the wind blows away. A beautiful picture of family life is found in Psalm 128 which begins with the same 'blessed' as the first Psalm. Verse 3 refers once again to the vine and the olive: 'Your wife will be like a fruitful vine within your house; your children will be like olive shoots around your table … Behold thus shall the man be blessed who fears the Lord.' The relationship between the individual and the community is a prefiguration of the spiritual health of individuals in faithful church fellowships in the New Testament.

The accent on separation

The people of God in both the Old Testament, and the believing community in the New Testament, are called to be different from those around them. We forget this feature of the biblical message because of the modern accent on individual diversity and social inclusion. This tendency has been

14. Cf. the vision of the golden lampstand and the two olive trees anointing it in Zechariah 3. The prophet, in line with Isaiah 4:2, calls the promised Saviour 'the Branch' in 2:8 and 6:12. In Revelation the seven gold lampstands represent the seven churches, a symbol of the people of God.

unwittingly reinforced in evangelicalism by the popularity of 'contextualisation' in theology and missions. Of course adaptation to culture is important in terms of 'being all things to all people' and being aware of cultural contexts. However, the accent of Scripture falls on the contrast between the life of faith and unbelief, obedience to God and following the crowd.

These are some big words, but follow along since it's quite practical. If 'contextualisation' is important, it is the case only as a subsidiary of 'decontextualisation'. The history of salvation continues the creational accent on separation for holiness. God calls and separates His people out from their surroundings to serve Him. The biblical model is not one of 'contextualisation'. It is firstly decontextualisation and then recontextualisation. Because of their difference the people of God are called to be a witness to those around them. 'What nation has a great God like this?' When the Lord commands His people, 'You shall have no other gods before me', that means not only 'you shall be different from the nations', but also 'you shall not return to the slavery and false gods of Egypt. I saved you from all that.'

Only by conscious separation is freedom real and growth possible in God's service. The thoughts and behaviour, the standards and goals of believers are made by God and not by what's trending in a changing world. Moreover, they are different because God has given promises that go way beyond the expectations of health and wealth in this world.

So when people say, as is often the case, 'we are in the twenty-first century and have to accept this or that' it's a red herring. Dean Inge rightly observed: 'Nothing is so reactionary as being up to date. Marry the spirit of your own generation and you will be a widower in the next.'[15]

---

15. William R. Inge, from his diary November 10, 1911. Charles H. Spurgeon said something very similar in one of his sermons, *The Metropolitan Tabernacle Pulpit: Sermons Preached by C. H. Spurgeon*

Jesus and God's new people

The second exodus of Israel was the return of the remainder of God's people after seventy years of captivity in Babylon, following the edict of Cyrus in 538 B.C. They returned through the desert and the second temple was built, as told by Ezra and Nehemiah. After the exile the people were less prone to idolatry, but legalism began to rear its ugly head.

The return from captivity became a model, against the backdrop of God's call of Abraham from Haran and the exodus from Egypt, for the final awaited liberation and the coming of the promised Messiah. John the Baptist's witness as the forerunner of Jesus was in terms of Isaiah's prophecy. He was the voice of one crying in the desert, which recalled the two great exoduses from exile: 'Make straight the way of the Lord'. Baptism for repentance prepared for the coming of the promised Christ.

In John 1:29-34 the witness of the Baptist is expressed in the three titles used to describe the expected Messiah: 'The lamb of God who takes away the sin of the world', 'he who baptises with the Spirit', and the 'Son of God'. Together they indicate that John was aware he stood on the cusp of a new age. Jesus, the Son of God will intervene to deliver His people from sin as their passover lamb in a new exodus. He will re-establish them by bringing in the promised age of the Spirit which will come when He is glorified, according to John 7:39. The people of God do not enter a new land, but Christ's kingdom, the new spiritual age which is dawning.

In Luke's account of the transfiguration, Jesus spoke with Moses and Elijah, the two great covenant leaders of the Old Testament who mysteriously appeared. They spoke about the

---

Revised and Published During the Year 1892, Vol. 38, Sermon Title: His Own Funeral Sermon, October 19, 1890.

'exodus' Jesus was about to accomplish at Jerusalem.[16] Jesus was conscious that He would fulfil the role assigned to Him by His forerunner. His death and resurrection bring God's kingdom and deliverance from sin. As risen Lord He will lead many captives to the freedom of a new life. Jesus fulfilled the exodus model by leading them into the realm of His new spiritual kingship, which announces a whole new future creation.

This double perspective of Jesus' action explains why people speak about the 'already' and the 'not yet'. The exodus to the new kingdom has *already* taken place. The complete unfolding in the new creation of righteousness is *not yet*, because it awaits Jesus' second coming. Summing up, Jesus brings the new exodus in several ways:

1. The first exodus was God's deliverance; as the Son of God Jesus brought God's liberation in a new personal way.
2. The exodus was from slavery to the freedom of sonship. Israel became God's son, His chosen one. Jesus' redemption from sin is adoption into God's people. Believers united to Jesus belong to Him.
3. Moses was a type of Jesus. He was chosen, called and empowered to be God's servant. As God's Son, Jesus received the Holy Spirit especially in His baptism (a symbol of the exodus) to achieve the work of salvation. He gave His Spirit baptism to form a new people at Pentecost.
4. The exodus was freedom for obedience and fruitfulness in the land. Jesus' new covenant people are planted in Him to be 'a chosen race, a holy nation, a people for his own possession', to proclaim the 'excellencies of him who called them out of darkness into his marvellous light'.[17]

---

16. Luke 9:31.

17. 1 Peter 2:9. Cf. 1:13-28.

5. The destination of the first exodus was the promised land; the second is Jesus' new creation, via the gathered New Testament community.

The biblical model of the Old Testament is reproduced in the new creation work of Jesus. He redeems from the slavery of sin, saves from a lost world, forms His people as a new community planted in Him, nourishes them, calls them to be fruitful through the Spirit He gives, and promises a new creation of justice and righteousness. The hope of a home in this new creation, prepared by Jesus Himself, should fill us with excitement, or as our forebears said, 'heavenly joy'.

Planting God's new covenant people

The most fundamental thing that can be said about the new covenant following Jesus' exodus is as follows. In the Old Testament, God's people were planted in the promised land to flourish there; in the New, God's children are planted in Christ to grow up to full stature in Him. That stature is ultimately reached when Christ returns, but its beginning is here and now. Desiring to grow in Christ and seeking to do so is the challenge of every Christian believer. If we don't take this seriously we end up struggling with false expectations or frustrations as we obsess about how we feel at this moment.

Because of the very nature of Jesus' saving work, the images the New Testament uses to teach about spiritual growth in Him are of a more personal nature than those in the old covenant. However, the goal of obedience to God and growth to fruitfulness remains a constant and the old images are integrated with new ones. The three major descriptions of new beginnings in Christ are, as might be expected, new creation, death and resurrection, and new birth.[18] Fundamental to all three is the idea of newness and being like Jesus, conformed to His pattern.

1. New creation in Christ

We have already referred to the fact that according to 2 Corinthians 5 anyone in Christ is a new creation with Him, because they get their identity from Him. In the previous chapter, in 2 Corinthians 4:6, the apostle Paul makes a surprising comparison:

> For God who said, 'Let the light shine out in darkness,' has shone in our hearts to give the light of the knowledge of the glory of God in the face of Jesus Christ.[19]

Several things strike us here. New life comes by the command of God who says 'let there be light', as He did when He created the world. Secondly, the light overcomes the darkness and pierces the void it hides. Nothing can be done in the darkness of sin, but when the light comes, new life flourishes. Thirdly, when you are in the sunlight you don't wish to return to 'hour of the wolf' darkness. Light is reassuring, darkness is scary. When the light is switched on it brings knowledge that radiates from the person of the Lord Jesus. This is close to what Paul says elsewhere about being transformed to the image of Christ. The light of Christ changes us to His likeness. It is both felt by us and perceptible to others. Finally, nothing is said here explicitly about the Holy Spirit and the Word of God. But the reference to light implies the work of the Spirit and the

18. I remember reading this years ago in Paul Helm's *The Beginnings*, (Banner of Truth Trust, 1986).

19. Cf. Ephesians 4:23-24 where Paul speaks about 'putting on the new self, created after the likeness of God in true righteousness and holiness.'

knowledge of Christ indicates the word of the gospel. More of that in a minute. For the present it's clear that new life in Christ is becoming a new creation in Him.

2. Death and resurrection with Christ

Dying to the past life and being raised with Christ in newness of life is a central theme in the New Testament. It's a vivid image, often associated with baptism. There are many references to it. Talking of His death in John 12:24 Jesus said:

> Truly, truly, I say to you, unless a grain of wheat falls into the earth and dies, it remains alone; but if it dies, it bears much fruit.

Once again the picture speaks volumes. Jesus' contemporaries all understood it since their livelihood depended on the mystery of planting and growth. A seemingly dead seed thrown in the ground surprisingly comes to life weeks later, sprouts and multiplies. From the one come many. Jesus will die and come to life again, and in doing so will germinate life in many others. His death will bear much fruit because many will be raised to life with Him.

Perhaps the best known passage about spiritual resurrection is found in Romans 6:1-11.[20] Paul says believers are 'dead to sin' and 'alive to God' in Jesus Christ. Verses 4-6 and 11, state Paul's argument:

> We were buried with him by baptism into death, in order that, just as Christ was raised from the dead by the glory of the Father, we too might walk in newness of life. For if we have been united with him in a death like his, we shall certainly

20. We will also refer to this in the next chapter but in terms of participating in Christ.

> be united with him in a resurrection like his … You must consider yourself dead to sin and alive to God in Christ Jesus.

What does this mean? Simply that by being one with Him by faith, what has happened to Jesus mysteriously happened to us in Him. Believers in Christ, as Colossians 3:1 states, 'have been raised with Christ (to) seek the things that are above, where Christ is, seated at the right hand of God.'

Ephesians 2:4-6 expresses the same idea:

> God being rich in mercy … when we were dead in our trespasses, made us alive together with Christ—by grace you have been saved— and raised us up with him and seated us with him in the heavenly places in Christ Jesus…

Sin and death have passed away and in Christ believers enter a new life. We are to see ourselves from this new perspective. By faith we are alive to, with, and in the Lord Jesus. God has spiritually raised us from the dead, like Him. It is nothing we have done, but it is God's work in us. True, we still live on this earth and are embroiled in a struggle to the death with sin; but our destiny is resurrection to new life that's already happened. What is a spiritual hope for faith today will be a physical and bodily reality in the future. The future resurrection to eternal life will happen in due course, when Christ returns.

3. New birth and regeneration

Resurrection with Christ happens by spiritual rebirth or regeneration. The expression 'born again' has passed into common usage to describe any life-changing experience. An alcoholic once told me she was born again when she did the A.A. programme, and she meant nothing Christian by it. So when people speak about 'new birth' we have to be careful.

The Christ-centred context is vital. Jesus Himself, according to Romans 8:17 and 29, is the firstborn of many heirs who are adopted with Him into God's family. In Titus 3:5 Paul also speaks about the washing of regeneration (*palingenesia*) and the renewal of the Holy Spirit. This indicates two aspects of new birth, a purification from sin and newness of life from God's Spirit.

John is on the same wavelength as Paul in the well-known passage in chapter 3:5-7 of his Gospel:

> Unless one is born of water and the Spirit he cannot enter the kingdom of God. That which is born of the flesh is flesh and that which is born of the Spirit is spirit … You must be born again.

Nicodemus, who was a teacher of Jewish law, must have got the message following Jesus' gentle chiding.[21] Rebirth always refers back to a point of origin.[22] Without it, it's impossible to enter God's kingdom, or even to 'see' it. That expresses three ideas about the new birth:

1. It is a radical life-changing event, necessary because the old life of sin leads to death.
2. If a person is converted or born again, it is only because of the renewing action of God's grace.
3. Human beings are passive in natural birth. So also they depend on divine intervention for the birth from above. We did not cast a vote for our natural birth; spiritual birth comes from God's decision and the work of His Spirit. John 3:8 says, 'the wind blows where it wishes' to describe

21. In rabbinic Judaism when proselytes become Jews they were considered as newly born children.

22. John 3:3, 5, 6, 7, 8. Four times in John's first Epistle the new birth is an act of God (*ek tou theou,* 1 John 2:29, 3:9, 4:7, 5:1).

the effective and sovereign nature of the Spirit's work in regeneration.

New birth, like creation and resurrection, is into a newness of life in Christ. Just as He was raised from the dead by the Spirit and declared to be the Son of God with power, so believers are born again by faith and adopted into Him when they are spiritually raised and become part of His new creation. These three ideas are inseparable to describe the broad sweep of the new reality into which faith in Christ ushers us. Sin, death and judgment are replaced by acceptance and life, because 'all things have become new'. To know Christ and His grace is to be known in Him.

To sum up with a wide-angle view. When the Lord Jesus came, He established His kingdom which is different from the world. He is the king who brought the kingdom of new beginnings: freedom from the slavery of sin and death. The nature of His kingdom is spiritual. Entry into it is by spiritual renewal: being born anew, a resurrection to life, with the hope of new creation. Those who are alive to God in Christ are together the 'body of Christ', the people of the new covenant.

Word and Spirit in beginnings

The pictures of new creation, death and resurrection and new birth are dramatic ways biblical revelation helps us to understand freedom from sin in Christ, models of the reality of spiritual renewal. As our eyes are opened to the radical nature of the change, God chooses to reveal His work in this way in order to adapt to our limited understandings. Whenever God acts in temporal and historical reality His presence and work are a mystery to us. What really happened? How did God do it? How could our heart-attitude to God be changed? Knowing it has happened is one thing, but when we try to answer these questions we don't get very far. For this reason the Holy Spirit chose to reveal God's work by using word pictures.

Is there anything more we can say about these beginnings? Well yes, we can take a further look at the relationship between the Word and the Spirit in their work of renewal. This question has tended to generate more heat than light, but really it's fairly straight forward. Think of people hearing the good news of salvation presented clearly for the first time. They hear the Word and, if they savingly believe, it means the Holy Spirit has also been at work. So both Word and Spirit are involved, but in what order? Which has priority? Does the Word work directly and the Spirit seal it by faith that follows? Or does the Spirit work prior to hearing the Word?

All this might seem like a chicken-or-egg question. In order to make sense of these questions, we must try to approach them biblically. Four considerations are useful for an understanding of the Word-Spirit relation.

1. Firstly, those hearing the good news are never just random 'persons'. They are always sinners who are blind, deaf, and dumb to God.[23] They might be the most brilliant people, but spiritually they're nothing but corpses. One can speak to a corpse for ever, and not get a reaction. Even the inspired Word of God, in all its truth is without effect, in the same way that Pilate was blind to the incarnate Truth standing before him. In both the parable of the sower and the two houses we have referred to, the Spirit prepares the way. The ground is broken up to receive the seed, and digging is done to lay the foundation. In a fallen world God's Spirit must have *logical* priority with regard to the Word, even though *temporally* both Spirit and Word may

23. The healing of the blind man by Jesus in John 9 is one long illustration of this fact.

operate simultaneously. The reason for this is because the Spirit is a 'pure' divine reality, whereas the inspired Word is 'mixed', being both divine and human. The power of the Word comes from the Spirit, both in biblical inspiration and personal regeneration.

2. Is there any biblical warrant for this? Obviously that's an important question. Two texts in particular are referenced, 1 Peter 1:23 and 1 John 3:9:

    > You have been regenerated, not by (*ek*) corruptible seed, but incorruptible, by (*dia*) the living and permanent word of God.

    > Whoever is born of God does not commit sin, because the seed of God dwells in him, and he cannot sin, because he is born of God.

    In the first text, Peter is not dwelling on how regeneration happens, but on its imperishable character. He distinguishes between the seed and the Word, despite their close relationship. This is seen in the difference of the two prepositions used. Believers are regenerated by (*ek,* out of) the imperishable work of the Spirit, but through (*dia,* through) the living Word of God. It's a fine distinction. The Word is the means by which regeneration takes place, but the Spirit-seed is the factor that prepares for it. Thus the Spirit is the *effective cause* of regeneration, the origin and principle of new life, whereas the Word is the *instrumental means* by which new birth takes place. Likewise, in 1 John 3:9 believers cannot 'sin to death' because they are reborn of God by the Spirit-seed.

3. Word and Spirit can never be separated. Both must be considered vital and are inseparable in the entering of new

life. This is the position of John Calvin presented in the *Institutes of the Christian Religion*:

> The Spirit of God is so joined together and united with the truth expressed in the Scriptures that his power is tangible when the word is received with due respect... The Lord has united and knit together the truth of his Spirit and of his word. When our understanding receives this word obediently we behold the light of the Spirit enabling us to behold the face of God. Also when without fear of error or of being in error we receive the Spirit of God we recognise him in his image, that is, in his word.[24]

Calvin maintains a fine balance; the Word is not separated from the Spirit, nor the Spirit from the Word. At the same time they are distinct from each other. Calvin does not address the 'chicken-or-egg' question. Perhaps it did not cross his mind like it did for later Reformed theologians who dug deeper into the subject in order to reply to human-centred views of conversion.[25]

4. Two dangers indicate why the question of the relation of Word and Spirit is important for beginnings. It has practical consequences. One of the two elements might be eclipsed by the other, rather than them being seen as complementary.

   If the Word is taken to be the prime factor in conversion, then argument and demonstration will be of great importance in preparing the way for the Spirit's work.

---

24. John Calvin, *Institutes of the Christian Religion*, I.9.3, my translation. This quotation expresses Calvin's Chalcedonian theology.

25. Including Charles Hodge, Robert L. Dabney, Abraham Kuyper, Herman Bavinck, Louis Berkhof and John Murray. Nearly all of them until recently come down on the side of 'immediate' regeneration, that is the Spirit acts in logically prior fashion to the word. Benjamin B. Warfield has a more 'coordinate' view of their dual action and is closer to Calvin.

The temptation is to insist on the place of good reasoning and logical demonstration for conviction. If the intellectual job is done well, the main work is done. This does not encourage direct dependance on the Spirit's work. It is also tempting to reduce belief simply to agreeing with a series of correct propositions to which we can sign up. But faith is most of all trust, confidence in Christ and assurance.

If, on the other hand, the Spirit is given pride of place, moving people to 'feel it' may take pole position. The temptation is to think that being serious with the Word is of secondary importance. Having the right feelings is the way to faith. Believing is all about impressions and feeling good about it. Illuminism is the danger to be avoided here. If conversion includes the illumination of the mind, and if faith is living trust in Christ, these are never separated in biblical truth.

This is why Calvin insisted on the two factor approach to beginnings. The spiritual awakening of saving faith is neither intellectual conviction nor illuminism. In the light of biblical teaching, we ought to distinguish it from both. Faith equally embraces both Word and Spirit. Nevertheless, because we are sinners the Spirit turns the switch changing our hearts and opening the eyes of our minds to embrace the truth of the Word.[26]

Life to death or Death to life?

Elton John's song 'Circle of life' in *The Lion King* says the wheel of fortune 'keeps great and small on the endless round'. This is

26. For further discussion on the relation of Word and Spirit with contrasting viewpoints see Stuart Olyott, *Something Must Be Known and Felt*, (Bryntirion Press, EMW, 2014), and Ralph Cunnington, *Preaching With Spiritual Power: Calvin's Understanding of Word and Spirit in Preaching*, (Christian Focus, Mentor, 2015).

a pagan view of life and a blatant lie. A circle has no beginning and no end, it's an eternal return, a karma-laden fantasy. It's untrue because naturally we die and fall off the circle of life which no longer exists for us. Many people imagine the circle goes on because we survive in people's memories. Deceased loved ones 'in the next room' somehow 'watch over them'. That's neither true nor satisfying. Woody Allen hit the nail on the head when he commented: 'I don't want to achieve immortality through my work; I want to achieve immortality through not dying. I don't want to live on in the hearts of my countrymen; I want to live on in my apartment.'

The Christian view of life is realistic even if it may seem harsh. We need weaning off the syrup of sentimental pap. Life is not a circle, but two lines: the first is life to death; the second is death to life which intervenes and crosses it.

Beginnings are vital. We are all on the line from life to death, like the whole human race going back to the first couple and original sin. Death is our human destiny, and it discriminates against nobody. However, this line is intersected by the death to life line. Jesus came into human existence to take our death upon Himself, and in dying He saved us for life with Him. He opened up the new creation in His resurrection, because He Himself is that new creation. In Him we have life, eternal life.

We start well on the path to Christian life when and if the beginning is right. We get off the path to death and onto the path of life that begins in Christ.

QUESTIONS FOR DISCUSSION

1. What is the importance of beginnings in the Christian life?
2. Indicate two important beginnings in the Bible that are the key to everything else.

3. What was the initial act of anti-creation in our world and the result of it?
4. How does Jesus bring a new beginning according to the Gospels? Why is this the focus of the Christian life?
5. How does God plant His people when He saves them?
6. What have you learned about vines and olives?
7. Why is decontextualisation from the world important?
8. Can you give three biblical images for being planted in Christ?
9. Describe your beginnings as a believer.
10. What is the relation of Word and Spirit in beginnings?
11. What's wrong about the 'circle of life'?

2

BEING ROOTED

Rooting is important
How rooting takes place in Christ
Grafted, partaking, and adopted in Christ
Taking Christian teaching seriously
It's all about God's acts
Knowing God more

Chapter theme: *The second stage of growth is the rooting of the planted seed. Believers are rooted in Christ. Like the branches of a vine they are grafted into Him and partake of His life. The life of Christ is theirs as it flows into them. This promotes stability and growth. Rooting in Christ means being grounded in God's people. Biblical doctrine is about the mighty acts of God in salvation. God saves and unites His people in Christ according to His eternal purposes. That is why biblical roots are vitally important.*

Planting is important, but it must be followed up by long-term rooting. Without proper roots plants are precarious. A dental implant may give a great smile, but if the jawbone root support is inadequate, it's goodbye to that with a steak dinner. Rooting is as essential to growth as planting because it promotes stability.

In presentations of the Christian life sometimes this question is a neglected subject. There is plenty of talk about sanctification and maturity, but not so much about rooting itself. Perhaps this explains why some people who make a profession of faith are uprooted and fall by the wayside. So in this chapter we will look at what it means to be rooted in Christ.

Being rooted is mentioned a few times in the later epistles of Paul:

> May (God the Father) grant you to be strengthened with power through his Spirit in your inner being, so that Christ may dwell in your hearts through faith—that you being *rooted and grounded* in love, may… know the love of Christ that surpasses knowledge, that you may be filled with all the fullness of God (emphasis added).

> As you received Christ Jesus the Lord, so walk in him, *rooted and built up* in him and established in the faith…[1] (emphasis added).

Rooting is the activity of Father, Son and Spirit, the divine trinity working together. The believer is *in* Christ Jesus the Lord, the heavenly risen Messiah. Rooting *comes from* the grace of God the Father and has as its goal 'the fullness of God'. It is done *by* the Holy Spirit. The Spirit brings Christ to us and us to Christ. He dwells in us by faith, and so we personally experience the love of Christ. By the work of the Spirit God

1. Ephesians 3:16-18, Colossians 2:6-7. See also Ephesians 2:21 where growing into Christ and being built together with Him is a whole church reality.

plants believers in Christ so that they are joined to Him and they know the joy of fellowship with Him.

We will firstly see the way the New Testament describes this and then the means the Spirit uses to deepen rooting in Christ.

One with Christ

The oneness of the believer and the Lord Jesus is presented in a bouquet of pictures by the New Testament. Christ lives and dwells in believers and they exist in Him like the head and the members of the body, the husband and wife, or the cornerstone and the building. These images express that Jesus united Himself to our humanity and as a result we are united to Him.

This relationship is described in a variety of ways. We will choose three: engrafting, participation and adoption. Being grafted into Christ roots us in Him. It describes the living union and the source of new life of believers in Christ. Participation in His life is fellowship (*koinōnia*) in His body. Adoption is an act of God that undergirds the fact that we are one with Christ.

The depth of the believer's relation to Christ expressed by these notions is illustrated by three central biblical texts.

Grafted into Christ: John 15:1-11

Believers are grafted into the true vine (v.1). Their vital sap, their spiritual life and strength, comes from Christ alone. Without Jesus, and apart from Him, they are nothing (v.5). United to Him they draw their vitality from Him. How does this happen?

Living for many years in southern France, I knew a few vineyard workers. So I learned a bit about wine production. An elder in one of the churches I visited was director of the local 'cave coopérative', a good source of both information and the product itself! Without grafting a vine remains 'wild' and will never produce edible grapes. It's fine for growing as shade on your porch, but no good for fruit. A fruitful vine is produced by making a cut in the rootstock, fitting the branch inside the cut and then binding it in. When Jesus said, 'I am the vine, you are the branches' the disciples would have understood exactly what that meant. Christ has to be 'cut' for us to be grafted in Him. So we are grafted into His death, and receive life from His resurrection in order to produce fruit.

Spiritual life flows from grafting, an image of being rooted in Christ. Believers are bound to Christ by faith as a result of the work of the Spirit. Three comments can be made:

- we have no life or power for good apart from Jesus, the vine;
- when rooted in Him we are cultivated and pruned by the Father, who is the 'vinedresser';
- fruit is borne by abiding in Christ and He in us, through the Spirit's work.

So fruitful vines are grafted into Christ, bound to Him by faith, and receive sap from rooting in Him. The Father is the vinedresser who plants us in Christ. Life in Christ begins when we take root in Him. Real life is not found elsewhere. Good fruit can only be produced by branches rooted in the true vine.

Being aware of the depth of this image helps us to realise what an enormous privilege it is to be part of Christ, to live in Him and to be daily strengthened by Him. The wonderful thing is that God is at work in us as Christ lives in us and the Spirit strengthens us. What peace and happiness this brings!

Taking part in Christ: Romans 6:1-11

We commented on Romans 6 in the previous chapter with regard to the beginning of new life. There is a further perspective. The apostle Paul describes how believers are joined together with Christ and participate in what He has done. In a spiritual way our experiences mirror and follow His. What happened to Him literally is reflected in us spiritually as our faith follows the pattern of His work and is modelled by it.

If you play a game you are joined with your game partners and share a common activity with them. What they do, you do, until the game ends. However, Paul's 'game' is not competitive but constructive. Christ always has the first move, and participating in it with Him, we react with and to Him.

Romans 6:2-8 describes some of the many and varied ways we are joined to Christ. Jesus cleanses us by dying for us and gives us new life by making us partakers with Him. When we are joined to Him the invisible power of His death and His resurrection life become real in us. We die and re-live with Him. New life in Christ gives hope of resurrection in Him. Baptism in Him admits us into sharing in His grace. This translates into the fact that we are dead to sin in Him and freed from its enslaving chains. Christians show evidence of participation in Christ's death by cross-bearing, in dying to sin. This is accompanied by newness of life which mirrors that in being joined to Christ we receive incorruptible life from Him.

Death to sin and new life in Christ for the believer are a bit like train tracks. Looking along the tracks we see they stretch together into eternity. One is never separate from the other, because Jesus paved the way for us.

The expressions Paul uses refer in one way or another to the death and resurrection of Christ and to our identity with Him in those once-for-all acts. He 'was delivered up for our trespasses and raised for our justification'.[2] His death destroys and demolishes the sinfulness of our flesh and the resurrection renews our inner nature. It's not possible to be united to Christ unless our sin is dealt with. When that's the case, we are justified from it by Him. When that happens Christ's sanctifying power of life flows into our lives. All this is because believers are joined with Christ and 'possess' Him.[3]

Cleansing from sin is the result of justification. Christ took God's judgment against us on Himself and paid the price to remove our sin. Newness of life is expressed in sanctification, growth in the grace of Christ. Believers have both these graces together, since they have Christ Himself and what belongs to Him. So you cannot, as a believer, have justification without sanctification, or sanctification without justification.[4]

That explains why Jesus could say to the dying thief on the cross, 'Today you will be with me in paradise.' Salvation is complete in Christ who saves us and God accepts us through the merits of Christ.[5] Our salvation is never more real, complete or perfect than it is now by faith in Christ through grace. Knowing this brings great assurance, in spite of our weakness and our continuing sinfulness. Christ's grace is the gift that never stops giving. Can you imagine anything more wonderful than that?

---

2. Romans 4:25.

3. John Calvin, *Institutes of the Christian Religion*, III.16.1. This 'possession' makes for a 'triangular' relation with Christ together with justification and sanctification.

4. Both justification and sanctification are by faith, but faith does not work in the same way in both cases. Justification is imputed (granted) to us when faith is present as its instrument, whereas sanctification is received by faith through the infusion of the Holy Spirit, working out the consequences of justification in us.

5. Christ's merits are complete through His active obedience (He lived the perfect life) and passive obedience (He died a sinless death). We are saved as much by one as the other.

Adoption in Christ: Romans 8:13-17

Union with Christ is the closest of relationships. When believers are grafted into Christ the vine, they participate in a shared life with Him because He indwells them. But there is more. By becoming one with Him, we also partake in His *status*. Nothing could root in Christ as securely as this.

So the intimacy of union with Christ also involves sharing His sonship. There is a link between union with Christ and adoption in Him as the result of justification. By nature we are not members of God's family but children of wrath.[6] In Christ we are adopted into the family and become sons of God. In justification we are pardoned by God the judge; in adoption we become sons of the Father because of the Son.[7]

Romans 8 follows on from the apostles' great chapters 5 and 6 on justification. It is a series of litmus tests that show the presence of new life and the assurance believers have in Christ. Trust in Christ comes through the leading of the Spirit who brings recognition of sonship: 'All who are led by the Spirit of God are sons of God (and) receive the Spirit of adoption as sons, by whom we cry "Abba, Father!"' (v.14, 16).

Assurance of faith comes from a special work of the Holy Spirit. The Spirit impresses on believers the fatherly grace of God who forgives all sins, past to future. The Spirit emboldens trust in prayer and believers cry out to the Father as sons. They are no longer slaves, and will not slip back into slavery, because now they are members of the household. That is their status and title.[8]

---

6. Ephesians 2:1-10.

7. Paul is talking about the legal aspect of sonship. 'Daughters' in Christ have the same legal status because they are 'sons' of God too, even if this may seem strange to us today.

8. Romans 8 from 'no condemnation' to 'nothing can separate us from the love of God in Christ Jesus' provides many reasons that encourage the assurance of believers.

Adoption to sonship is the special work of the Holy Spirit which roots believers in Christ. Salvation includes not only having God as Father but also being adopted by Him as His children. More wonderful still, inheritance is held in common with the Son. Believers are sons of God with the Son. When the Father considers their place He sees them as being one with His own Son. Jesus is the natural Son, believers are God's sons and heirs by adoption.

There is a rider in verse 17: 'fellow heirs with Christ, provided we suffer with him in order that we may also be glorified with him'. God's inheritance is ours because by His grace He has adopted us to be His children. We are called to enter into the inheritance as partners with Christ by following His sacrificial model.

There is an observable order to the Christian life. Because of redemption accomplished by the Son, the Spirit of adoption is given. The experience of assurance of salvation by faith, of the struggle against sin, of trust and prayer, comes with the witness of the Spirit. These realities make the believer one with Christ in His inheritance.

Putting roots down

Grafting, participation in Christ and adoption make us children of God. But is there anything in the rooting image that we must do? Surely we are not simply passive? How do we, as believers, own this rooting and make it ours?

There is a lead to answer this question in John 15. In verse 3, talking about the pruning of the branches, Jesus says to the disciples, 'You are already clean because of the word that I have spoken to you' (NIV). One possible meaning of this is that the disciples had already experienced pruning when they were grafted into Christ. Like shoots they were cleansed or pruned by

Christ's word. The truth of the gospel is like a vinedresser's knife that removes what prevents rooting. The cleansing power of the word Jesus spoke to His disciples helps ingrafting so that the sap of the vine can pulsate into the branches. Fruitful branches are grafted into Christ by being rooted in His teaching.

The teaching or doctrine of Christ, instruction in the meaning of His redemptive person and work, is vital for taking root in the faith and the stability that comes from it. Sound biblical teaching is the means the Spirit uses to root believers in Christ. We are called to receive it, apply it to ourselves and rejoice in so that we are firmly rooted in Him.

The usual suspect

Mention the word doctrine in some circles and people go into tailspin. They are allergic to the idea of doctrine, immunised against it, and even more so to dogma, which is associated with Catholicism. They feel their faith rather than think it. 'Head knowledge' is dangerous. To diminish the prejudice I will use biblical 'teaching'.

There are many reasons for this suspicion, some understandable, others less so. Liberal theology has had the quasi-monopoly of Christian soundbites for well over a century. Leaders of the mainline churches have followed its slippery paths to unbelief and now embrace wokeism without hesitating. These are the people who get quoted in the media. C.S. Lewis documented their critical attitude to biblical faith in his 1959 essay 'Fern seeds and elephants'. He attacked critical theologians who 'claim to see fern seed and can't see an elephant ten yards away in broad daylight.' A specialist of myths, Lewis thought that the critics who call the Bible myth have little idea what myths are and how they work.

Add to this the fact that the ecumenical movement promotes the attitude 'doctrine divides, service unites', a catchphrase that spread like an oil flack on a moving sea. These attitudes sourced an understandable fear of intellectualism among evangelicals. Furthermore, many suspect that theology itself is a risky business. The temptation is to bypass the lurking wolves by being practical about any issue from the word go. Theology is suspect of being more divisive than unitive—a kind of Trojan horse to smuggle unbelief into faithful churches.

Many young people from evangelical backgrounds lack backbone in biblical teaching. They are quite unprepared and succumb unconsciously to the post-truth values promoted by their education and milieu. Since they have no roots in biblical teaching they tend to drift away because of the 'intersectional' ethical difficulties they face.

The acronym MTD was coined to define the religious and spiritual attitudes of American teenagers, but it applies to the West in general: Moralistic, Therapeutic and Deistic. MTD means tolerance, compassion for all and doing good, feeling better about oneself, and an absent God who leaves you lots of freedom to get on with it. Because you want to be nice, God must be nice too, forgiving everything and everyone. It's about as far from John Bunyan's *Pilgrim's Progress* as east is from west, and the two have little in common.

However, the usual suspect, 'abstract theology', is no suspect at all. Theology, or Christian teaching, is not the cause of the problems evangelicals have with spiritual growth. On the contrary, it's the absence of teaching and biblical rooting that makes people go astray. It's also a lack of seriousness about biblical teaching. Conflicts in churches are more often about power struggles and personal ambitions than about doctrinal questions.

This should not really surprise us. Even in apostolic times there were those who, like children, were 'tossed to and fro by the waves and carried about by every wind of doctrine, by human cunning, by craftiness in deceitful schemes.' Sounds like the woke were at work then too! Paul's remedy was not openness therapy but more teaching. 'Rather speaking the truth in love, we are to grow up in every way into him who is the head, into Christ.'[9]

And you can only grow into Christ if your roots are deep in His realistic and loving teaching. So what is biblical doctrine or teaching, and how can we overcome prejudices against it? The main way of doing this is to correct false ideas about it.

Taking Christian teaching seriously

Biblical teaching is the most precious thing we can own. With it we think the same thoughts as God at our human level. That is why we should be deadly serious about it. Biblical teaching, not football, is more important than life and death. Nothing should demand our attention more. I run into people in churches who are ignorant about Bible teaching but they seem to think that they know enough : 'I've known all that since Sunday school.' We can be so familiar with it that it becomes faded. Or even worse, we imagine we can just do without it.

We have to realise that biblical teaching and theology are two different things. They are like two circles that touch, but it's important to distinguish them. The Bible's teaching presents what it means to believe in God as Creator and Saviour. It is fundamental, essential and necessary to rooting Christian faith and life. God reveals His truth in the Scriptures so we can get a grip on it. Biblical texts speak to everyone, are acceptable by all, and relevant to all. Even if some fine points escape us and some

9. Ephesians 4:14, 15.

parts of the Bible are a challenge, the basic message is clear. One of the great twentieth century Reformed theologians, Abraham Kuyper, was converted early in his pastoral ministry by the witness of a young Dutch peasant called Pietronella Baltus, who would not shake Dr Kuyper's hand because he was an unbeliever. Even though she was an uneducated country lass, she had understood the gospel, and she knew that Kuyper, a doctor in theology from a famous university, had not an inkling of what it meant.

'Doctrine' refers to the teachings of Scripture that are God's revelation to direct the life of His people. The word (*didaskalia*) appears more than twenty times in the New Testament. But a multitude of words convey the same idea: the gospel, wisdom from on high, message, testimony, truth, word of truth, deposit, instruction, sound words and the faith. It's a very broad notion. Believers are encouraged to follow 'good doctrine', to be nourished by it, established in its truth and to 'abide in the teaching of Christ'. Apostolic doctrine is the rule of faith for the Church both in preaching (*kērygma*) and instruction (*didachē*).[10] Believers are often warned against the perversions of human power or wisdom that oppose God and undermine biblical truth.[11] These warnings are so frequent that we can hardly think that the danger has disappeared today.

Biblical teaching is the means the Holy Spirit uses to root God's people firmly. It does so in four ways.

Firstly, biblical teaching, its doctrine, *gives a framework for understanding what life's about*: what we know about God, ourselves and others. The Bible provides a narrative about the

10. 2 Timothy 3:16 (*didaskalia*). See 1 Timothy 4:6, 6:20, 2 Timothy 1:12-14, Titus 1:9, 2:1, 7, 10, 2 John 9. Negatively, the warnings of Romans 16:17, Ephesians 4:14, 1 Timothy 1:10 and 6:3.

11. See what Isaiah says in 40:24 about princes and rulers who oppose God.

reality in which God has placed us and what He has done for us in both creation and redemption. As such it is life structuring. Biblical teaching is not a 'theory'; it gives us understanding of how God sees the world. The discernment it brings makes a difference between believers and unbelievers, in our way of looking at the world, not primarily through our feelings.

Secondly, doctrine *is useful because what it proposes is the truth.* It expresses God's version of who God is, what He has done, why we are here, and what our problems are. Take for example what is stated in 2 Corinthians 5:19, 'In Christ God was reconciling the world to himself.' What does it tell us? It's a doctrinal statement (or proposition) that presents several truths, gift-wrapped for us:

- God (Father, Son and Spirit) is personal and acts in Jesus Christ;
- Christ in the incarnation is the real presence of God in the world;
- when Christ acts, it is God who acts through Him;
- the result of God's action is forgiveness and peace;
- the beneficiaries are people with their needs (the 'world').

So one simple phrase is chock-full of teaching accessible to anyone. You don't have to be a high-flyer to find meaning for your life. Everyone can find it through the truth of God made known in Christ and all He has accomplished.

Thirdly, Christian teaching *is prophetic and apostolic.* In John 17:17-21, Jesus prayed for His disciples to be sanctified by the Word of God and by its truth. The Father sent the Son into the world to bring this truth; the Son sent His disciples, anointed by His Spirit, to transmit the same truth. Their word is received by 'those who believe' which binds them to Jesus in His truth. There is a chain of transmission. As believers we access God's truth by believing the apostolic teaching of the New Testament. By believing it we access the truth of Jesus proclaimed. That pleases the Father, who is well pleased with the Son. This is the way to be rooted in the message of Scripture. We receive it and believe it through the illuminating work of the Holy Spirit. With the help of the Spirit we can also tell the difference between truth and error.

Finally, there is *a sort of theology in the Scriptures.* We talk about the theology of Isaiah, John or Paul, but they are not really like present-day academic theologies. The inspired writers have their place in biblical revelation with their individual and collective understandings. God communicates His own truth through them. Biblical teaching bears witness to its truth because Scripture is the Word of God. It depends on the Holy Spirit as its guarantee, unlike other teachings that are merely human ideas. Biblical teaching has a unity that promotes the confession of a coherent faith and assurance regarding its truthfulness. In order to be rooted as a Christian you need to plunge deeply into God's truth revealed in Christ and His witnesses to get all you can out of it.[12]

Biblical teaching is practical

One of the suspicions people have about theology is that it creates an ivory towered luxury, far from the struggles of real life. True, theological debates are sometimes removed from reality. For instance, one evening in the year 1067, in the monastery of Monte Cassino in Italy (the site of a bloody battle in 1944), two monks had a pleasant chat. They discussed the surprising statement made by the church Father Jerome that

12. See the annexe which provides some practical suggestions about how Bible reading and prayer help us to be rooted in Christ.

even though God can do everything, he couldn't make a girl who has lost her virginity a virgin again!

Biblical teaching is a world away from that kind of monkish speculation. It's immediately practical in and of itself. It directly concerns how we view God, ourselves, and the world. We don't have to beat our brains to make it practical or to find how it applies to us. Knowing God is practical in and of itself, because it's loving Him and His truth.

This is the case because biblical teaching is divinely authorised spiritual truth. Without the testimony of the Holy Spirit, it's a labyrinth. Unbelievers might understand some of it, but they either have no insight into what it means, or they reject it as sheer madness.[13] Biblical teaching is part of the reality of the new world believers enter by the new birth. It's spiritual, it describes invisible things that are out of bounds for anyone without faith. It tells what a Christian is in a way human reasoning cannot grasp. The unbeliever has no understanding of biblical truth, like a colour-blind person who can only see grey.

Christian truth defines life. It brings us spiritually closer to God on God's terms. It allows us to see things as He sees them. It is the most precious reality we have in this life, where everything else passes away.[14] It makes us actors in the new creation united to the risen Christ. It gives us a glimpse of eternity. As believers, we should desire biblical teaching to root ourselves and to help others be rooted in the same faith. Paul encouraged Timothy in a letter to 'do his best to present himself to God as one approved, a worker who has no need to be ashamed, rightly handling the word of truth'.[15] That was

---

13. Like the Roman governor Porcius Festus did in Acts 26:24 when he shouted at Paul 'you are out of your mind'.

14. Isaiah 40:6-8.

15. 2 Timothy 2:15.

Timothy's particular responsibility. But Paul's exhortation is not limited to leaders alone. They are not a special case. All believers have the same calling.

At this point the question crops up: How do we put our finger on the relation between biblical teaching and theology? If they touch like two circles how are they similar and different?

Biblical teaching and theology

Some readers might not feel much concerned about theology, so we will move it along fast.[16] Obviously theology can be good or bad. It's good if it lines up with biblical teaching, and bad if it does not. So let's try and see how theology and biblical teaching are both important, how they are alike and different.

I think it's a question of level. A believer may well have a good knowledge of the teachings of Scripture but not be able to fit them together to make a complete picture. All the pieces are laid out like a jigsaw puzzle, but they have not been pieced together. So their unity is not apparent. Once the biblical teachings are assembled, a theological picture starts to appear.

All who believe in Scripture as the Word of God have some kind of theology. It may be at an elementary level or at a much higher level. The difference is like the one between a child doing a ten-piece jigsaw and an adult doing a thousand-piece puzzle. Both are challenged by their puzzle. All Christians are in some way theologians. We start being theologians when we try to answer questions like, 'Why do you believe Jesus can save you?', 'Who do you believe Jesus was?' or, 'What do you believe about God?'

Theology has to be rooted in biblical teaching, and express its meaning. It not only has the task of presenting a coherent

16. It's not to be forgotten that 'theology' means word of God or word about God.

picture of the Christian faith. It also has to present biblical teaching in different cultures, at different times and to different levels of audience. The theological understanding of the peasant woman who challenged Abraham Kuyper might have been elementary contrasted with the faith of an Augustine, a Calvin, or an Owen. But she knew why she was right and why Kuyper was wrong. In that sense she understood Scripture better than he did, and was more of a theologian than he was, with all his education. She was aware she couldn't convince him, but she told him to read Calvin, who did. So with the illumination of the Holy Spirit Kuyper's blind eyes were opened and he came to see the truth.

Theology is the application of biblical teaching seeking answers to questions in different situations. It is useful if it lines up with biblical teaching. If not, it may be worse than useless. Every biblical believer should be able to tell a heresy when they see one. For this reason, a distinction between biblical teachings and theology derived from them is useful.

Human theological ideas never have the normative character of biblical teaching. Even the confessions of the Church's faith are under the sole authority of Scripture. Final authority belongs to God alone and to His revealed Word. All other authorities or opinions are secondary and subject to them. So when a bigwig in the church says that the teaching of the Bible is homophobic we can shrug it off. On what authority are they stating that? Only that of their own opinion. Worse, they have a wolf's head on a sheep's body.

An example from John 3:16

The difference between biblical teaching and theology is one of level. The first is immediately accessible in what Scripture says, it is more direct and more easily checked out. Theology is a step removed from what the Bible says. It's more indirect and it's more of a challenge to check whether it's biblical or not. There is a lower margin for error in the interpretation of what the Bible teaches, but in theology it is far greater, because theological constructions are more complex.

We can illustrate the difference with reference to John 3:16: 'For God so loved the world that he gave his only Son, that whoever believes in him should not perish but have eternal life.'

What it teaches is pretty straightforward for all to see. It's not rocket science to get what John is saying. As biblical teaching it's clear. God loved the world in such a way and He gave His only Son. When anyone believes in Him the outcome is eternal life, not perdition. That is the Bible teaching. Of course it could be formulated differently, but it's easy to see if someone is wrong in how they understand it. Young and old, persons of all levels of intelligence, different cultures and times, can all commit to it. The Bible is written in such uncomplicated language that its major teachings are accessible to all, even though they may be very deep. No one is excluded because it's beyond them.

However, even when unbelievers do understand, they wriggle out of the challenge to believe in Jesus. They don't *want* to believe, they have no time for 'religion', they don't accept that Jesus or God exist, they make jokes about being born again, or worry that if they commit to Jesus they will be manipulated in some subtle way. Perhaps it just seems too easy and they want to do something hard, like begging 24/7 in the lotus position or making a pilgrimage somewhere. Or perhaps those who have worked very hard to get to where they are now, and who have always had to work to get anything they have in life, find it hard to accept that all they need to do trust in Christ. They think they need *to do* something, work at something to gain salvation.

At a theological level deeper questions are considered. First of all, did Jesus Himself say these words, or was this John's comment about His teaching to Nicodemus? Moreover, what did John mean when he used the words 'God', the 'world', 'believing', 'perishing' and 'eternal life'? How does his understanding fit in with that of the other New Testament writers? Personally, I think this text is John's comment on Jesus' teaching, but I could be wrong. 'God' means God the Father, the 'world' is the whole fallen creation, 'believing' indicates faith which is a gift of God, and 'eternal life' is something that begins here and now and stretches into eternity, forever. However, there are different answers to all these questions. I do not pretend that I have got them all right. A good commentary on John might put me straight if I consulted it!

Furthermore, John 3:16 can also be presented in a broader and deeper biblical perspective. It has a covenantal ring. God is the giver of eternal life; He gave His Son to that end as mediator; God promises salvation; faith is the condition for receiving it.

Finally, philosophical language could also be used to explain the relation between God's grace and faith in Christ, which is unmerited. John Calvin approaches John 3:16 by speaking of God as the source of salvation and Jesus Christ as the instrument to achieve it. He comments: 'The first place is assigned to the love of God as the sovereign cause or source; then follows faith in Christ as the second and more proximate cause.'[17] This explanation, all will agree, is quite a distance from the biblical teaching of the text. However, as a theological explanation of what it means, it's not wrong. What Calvin says neither contradicts the simple language of biblical teaching, nor

17. John Calvin, *Institutes of the Christian Religion*, II.17.2, my translation. See the argument on salvation by grace not works in III.14.17. Calvin rarely uses philosophical language but he does with relation to John 3:16 in these two cases. See also his commentary on this text.

its more covenant structured meaning presented above. It is good and legitimate theology, even though we might not be over-keen on the Reformer's use of language about 'causes'.

So on first level there is the simple and direct language of the Bible that God has used to reveal Himself. When we read it we understand and take in what the Bible teaches as truth. We can formulate its teachings or doctrines. Then there is theology, which is at a deeper level of explanation and complexity. All believers are encouraged by Scripture to deepen their knowledge of God's ways. As they do so they root deeper and deeper in God's Word and begin to grow stronger and stronger by being rooted in Christ. Without this rooting they can easily be blown over by the winds of human ideas that whistle around.

Believers are also called upon to examine themselves. This activity implies an examination of our rooting in Christ. The goal is to see whether the truth of Scripture is true of us. 'Examine yourselves, to see whether you are in the faith. Test yourselves. Or do you not realise this about yourselves, that Jesus Christ is in you?—unless indeed you fail to meet the test!'[18] We line ourselves up with what Scripture teaches to see if our rooting in Christ is solid.

Biblical teaching is about what God does

What is it about the teachings of the Bible that root us in Christ? Is there anything special that gives them the means to do this?

A popular theologian of the last century said that our relationship with God is a personal and living experience.[19] 'I' and 'you' indicate how God talks to us and we talk to Him. However, when we move into the realm of teaching about God (the dreaded 'doctrine') something takes place. We flip

18. 2 Corinthians 13:5, 2 Peter 1:10-11.

19. I am referring to the Swiss neo-orthodox theologian Emil Brunner.

from the intimate to the abstract realm. From the personal 'I' and 'you' to impersonal statements about God, 'he/she/it' is … This idea made a mark with many people. It stoked suspicion that Christian teaching is abstract and not personal. I don't think that's right and will explain why. Basically it's a misunderstanding about how God reveals Himself and what the teaching of Scripture is.

How does God teach us through His Word? God is not like a schoolteacher spoon-feeding pupils what they need to know to pass an exam. Nor are the teachings of Scripture random information to be found by doing a bit of digging in the Bible. Accessing the Bible is not like getting information from Wikipedia. The major teachings of Scripture are all about what *God has done*, or about things directly related to what He has done. Read Psalm 145 which demonstrates this! It's a wonderful acrostic centering on the incomparable nature of God's acts, acts that describe the nature of God's kingdom and make His name known.[20] The central verses are:

> All your works shall give thanks to you, O Lord,
>   and all your saints shall bless you!
> They shall speak of the glory of your kingdom
>   and tell of your power.

Meditating on the mighty acts of God focuses us on the steadfast love of God. The Lord is worthy to be praised!

When we describe biblical teachings, we are saying something about God and His acts. For that reason the teaching of the Bible has special power to instruct us and edify as 2 Timothy 3:16 states. All biblical teaching is rooted in God's actions either before, during, or after the biblical history of salvation: in creation, providence, salvation and new creation.

20. An acrostic Psalm is one in which each part begins with a letter of the Hebrew alphabet.

Note the verbs (words of action) in the following examples of well-known doctrines:

- Biblical revelation is God *revealing* Himself in both words and deeds;
- the counsel of God is God *deciding* future events and how they will happen;
- divine election is God *choosing* His people;
- providence is God *overseeing* creation and history, providing for and sustaining it;
- creation is God *making* all things, visible and invisible;
- sin speaks of God *judging* human rebellion;
- redemption is God *paying the price* for our freedom in Christ;
- justification is the act of God *declaring us righteous* on the ground of the perfect obedience of Jesus, condemned in our place;
- the return of Christ is His *coming* to bring in the new creation.

So when we are thinking about biblical teaching we must not focus primarily on 'the doctrine of x, y, z' but on God's acts, on what He does concretely. Doctrines are the by-products of God's acting.

In the teachings of biblical revelation we see that God is a living, personal God. God's actions are true and real, holy, loving and just. There is nothing impersonal about them. This is true even of the doctrine of the Trinity; God is three distinct persons but with one divine nature. The Father is God, the Son is God and the Spirit is God. A good many people have difficulty with this and say that 'trinity' is not even a biblical word. They think it's a mathematical impossibility. How can one be three and three be one at the same time? So they end up rejecting it as mumbo jumbo.

However, if we think that the biblical teaching about the Trinity presents what God *does* because He *is* God, we can begin to grasp it a little better, even though the nature of God is always mysterious to us. As Father, God *sends* His only Son; the Son in agreement *comes* to earth to reveal the Father and do His will; the Spirit *bears witness to* the Son and *comes from* the Father and the Son. The active relationships show that each of the persons is God. Together they act out of love in harmony with each other.[21] The Trinity is at work in the particular divine acts done by each of the persons in agreement with the others.

Biblical teaching is far from being an abstraction, but it brings us into contact with reality, with God, created meaning, the anguish of sin, the joys of salvation, the hope we need, and the love we long for. That's something we find only in Scripture and nowhere else. On the other hand, if we close our eyes to biblical teaching, we go on in the obscurity of our own ideas or, more often than not, those of others, disconnected from reality, condemned by our guilt and disillusioned by false hope.[22]

Let's illustrate further the idea that the teaching of the Bible involves God's actions. Martin Luther said that the doctrine of justification by faith alone is the central teaching of the Christian faith. He called it 'the material norm' (the content of faith) and Scripture the 'formal norm' (the structural principle of faith). However, not a few people find it difficult to assimilate justification into their understanding and apply it to daily life.

---

21. 1 John 4:8. In his treatise *On the Trinity* Augustine used an illustration: The lover (God the Father) loves the beloved (Jesus, the Son) in love (Holy Spirit).

22. 1 John 1:1-5.

They see it as legal, abstract, and a little elusive. Their personal experience ('I'm born again') seems more real.

How then can we think about justification and the crucial fact that God accepts us? We must think biblically and concretely about it, because justification is above all an act of God. The following pointers underpin justification as God's act:

- God is just in His judgment against sin;
- sin requires condemnation by God;
- Christ was condemned, the 'just for the unjust';
- justification is the opposite of condemnation;
- God justifies sinners by the 'glorious transfer'—what is ours (our sin) is counted (imputed) to Christ, and what is His (His righteousness) is counted to us;
- faith itself does not justify us before God; only the righteousness of Christ received by believing in Him justifies sinners.

Now re-read all of the above putting 'my' and 'me' in the statements. All that is true in general is true of each of us personally, through faith in Christ, when we belong to Him. This is the reality that defines our identity. What we think about ourselves guides how we feel about ourselves rather than the opposite. I may wake up on Monday morning in a funk about the week ahead, but I am not who I am because of what may happen to me in the hours or days ahead. Instead, my identity rests in God who has accepted me in Christ. I am not alone facing whatever happens, but a free person in Christ. Nothing will happen to me outside of the loving embrace of my Lord. That God has accepted us means He will care for us. We can never be more acceptable to God than the moment we first believed, because justification is God's active decision about us.

What God has done becomes our history and the story of our lives. This way of looking at biblical teaching can be applied to everything that the Bible teaches, as true about us, together with all God's children. Bible teaching is identity defining. People who are sniffy about it (or doctrine and good theology for that matter) are walking past the smorgasbord God has set out for their enjoyment and nourishment.

Rooting is about knowing God

How can we know more of God? There are several ways in which the teachings of the Bible help us to do so.

Firstly, the starting point of our knowledge of God may seem strange. It is simply that, naturally speaking, God is unknown to any of us. Without Scripture we might have some vague notions that there is a God, and some sense of what is right and wrong. But fundamentally we are in ignorance, as we have never met God. We are seated in the dark on the bleachers with the agnostics and Christianity's cultured despisers. In our finer moments, or in dire distress, we may rouse from our Netflix torpor to seek God. We try making altars for the 'unknown God'.[23] These idols are born of fear and end up being costly. A former Hindu in Bali told me that when he became a Christian he was better off, because he didn't have to offer sacrifices in his home and work to his gods every day. That God is naturally unknown means that there is no consensus about who God is, which is an undisputed fact for all around us.

Secondly, we know God by His attributes. Knowing God depends on a gracious act on God's part. When God makes Himself known He does so by His acts and His Word. Together

23. Acts 17:22-23. 'Religious' can also be translated 'superstitious'.

they explain His gracious intentions. In His revelation God shows Himself to be powerful, wise, present, and merciful.[24] In Psalm 119, the Word of God itself has many of the attributes of God. His Word is just (9x), marvellous (2x), true (6x), eternal (3x), upright (3x) and life-giving (v. 93).

As we have seen, God makes Himself known by His *acts*, which in turn display His personal *attributes*, what He is like. Knowing God's attributes we know God, not in Himself, which is impossible, but as He is in His salvation. Only the God of the Bible has these attributes.

Thirdly, the knowledge of God cannot be separated from knowing God as Saviour. This is underlined, in Deuteronomy 29:29, by the distinction between the things that are hidden in God and those that are revealed:

> The secret things belong to the LORD our God, but the things that are revealed belong to us and to our children forever, that we may do all the words of this law.

In Hebrews 1:1-3 the writer builds on this distinction to show how God has revealed Himself:

> Long ago, at many times and in many ways, God spoke to our fathers by the prophets, but in these last days he has spoken to us by his Son, whom he appointed the heir of all things, through whom also he created the world. He is the radiance of the glory of God, and the exact imprint of his nature, and he upholds the universe by the word of his power.

The apostle Paul is more economical in his terse statement in 1 Timothy 2:5:

24. God is powerful, Isaiah 55:8-11, Hebrews 4:12-13; wise, Psalm 33:4-5, 6-9; present, Deuteronomy 30:11-14, Romans 10:6-8; merciful, Isaiah 40.

> There is one God, and there is one mediator between God and men, the man Christ Jesus, who gave himself as a ransom for all.

The things we know about God, which are revealed, are known because Jesus is 'the radiance of God's glory', and 'the one mediator' of the knowledge of God and His salvation. In this way, we know God's acts and words which in turn present the attributes of God. They are supremely summed up in Jesus the mediator, whose mission was to reveal God and His will to us.[25] God makes Himself known by radiating knowledge of Himself in Christ's person and works.

Do we really and truly know God? Many people doubt that it's possible. We can only know things in this universe, which is a closed shop, and not outside it. But if what we have said about God revealing His attributes is right, we do really and truly know God. There is more. The attributes of God are *names* of God. When the Lord showed who He is to Moses He gave himself a name:

> The LORD, the LORD, a God merciful and gracious, slow to anger, and abounding in steadfast love and faithfulness, keeping steadfast love for thousands, forgiving iniquity and transgression and sin, but who will by no means clear the guilty visiting the iniquity of the fathers on the children.[26]

The whole of this declaration is a combined name of God. Moses bowed down and worshipped. He recognised that this is the eternal Lord. In a similar way all the attributes of God present names by which God is known. God is eternal, holy, and true. Put the definite article before the attribute and it

---

25. John 17:1-5.

26. Exodus 34:6-7. The reference to fathers and children does not mean, I think, that God punishes children for what they have not done, but refers to the social consequences of sin being inherited by descendants as it spreads.

becomes a name of God. He is the eternal God, the holy God, the God of truth. God loves because He *is* love.

Conclusion

Reading the Bible with the help of the Holy Spirit opening our eyes and revealing the truth discerning its teachings, beginning to delve into it, builds a constructive knowledge of God. The high point of this knowledge is the Lord Jesus Christ. Once we latch onto the concreteness of this and the wonder of God's grace, we will not let it go. True knowledge of God appreciates His grace and wonders at it. Our roots grip tenaciously to salvation in Christ as they penetrate deeper into God's eternal love.

Biblical teaching is not an end in itself, but a means to a greater end: that we may know God in whom is life eternal. Ultimately that is the reason why biblical roots are vitally important.

QUESTIONS FOR DISCUSSION

1. Why is 'rooting' important in the Christian life as well as 'planting'?
2. How are believers rooted in the Christ?
3. Indicate three biblical illustrations for 'rooting'.
4. What is the difference between biblical teaching and theology?
5. What are the prejudices against biblical teaching?
6. How is biblical teaching founded on the acts of God?
7. What is the link between God's acts and our knowledge of Him?

8. What is the importance of the attributes of God?
9. Why is knowing God important for 'rooting'?
10. How solid are your roots?
11. How can you become more serious about this?

3

GROWING UP

From childhood to adulthood
Progressive development
The importance of the big picture
Thinking God's thoughts after Him
Our limits and paradoxes

Chapter theme: *The third aspect of growth is steady development. Growth takes place when sap flows into the branches, buds appear, blossom breaks out, leaves grow and fruit ripens. Growth in grace comes through an increasing understanding of the wonder of God's salvation. We are 'mentored' by the big picture of salvation presented by the developing storyline of Scripture. We grow by 'thinking God's thoughts after Him' as we learn to piece together the pieces of the Bible picture.*

Some time in 1905 Lenin concluded that Trotsky was a bit light on Marxist orthodoxy and advised him to get to know Marx and Engels better. Lenin did not consider revolutionary practice enough. Trotsky lacked grounding in the doctrines of the party. Stalin later made short work of the maverick Trotsky when he was exiled in Mexico. Marxists obviously take their 'theory' very seriously, but do Christians have the same respect for biblical teaching?

When the apostles pray for believers they often pray for their growth in love and knowledge of the truth, in spiritual wisdom and understanding.[1] Is a lack of knowledge of the fundamentals of the Christian faith taken too lightly? Do churches really do the job they're supposed to—that is instructing people and giving them a backbone in biblical teaching? That alone can help believers grow in what they believe in order to stand up to the storms of life. The present-day Church tends to be light on teaching in spite of the profusion of ways and means.

At the end of his second epistle the apostle Peter leaves the following exhortation: 'Grow in the grace and knowledge of our Lord and Saviour Jesus Christ.' This echoes his opening salutation: 'May grace and peace be multiplied to you in the knowledge of God and Jesus our Lord. His divine power has granted to us all things that pertain to life and godliness, through the knowledge of him who call us to his own glory and excellence.'[2] If grace and knowledge are linked with growth, how exactly do they move it on from the initial planting and the subsequent rooting? We'll try to answer that question in this chapter.

Rooting is down and out into the earth, and visible upward growth is proof of hidden vitality. Normal trees spread their roots out to two or three times the extent of the branches, and

1. Philippians 1:9, Colossians 1:9, 2 Thessalonians 1:3, James 1:5.
2. 2 Peter 3:18. See also 1:2-3, 8, 11, 2:20.

in dry conditions up to five times. The concealed roots are important for stability; growth above ground shows all is well below.

God the Father plants and roots believers in Christ and makes them partakers in the blessings of sonship and His inheritance. Our life is personally grounded in God's story of salvation and we gain stability from being part of God's people. Growth is increasingly visible as we learn more of Christ. Fruit will appear by the work of the Holy Spirit.

Everything has its place in growth and develops over time. When we lived in the south of France we had a favourite walk we called 'the cherry tree walk'. At different seasons we observed the development of almond, cherry and olive trees and also vines. Almonds were the first to blossom, early February, cherries in April with the fruit ready by mid-June. Olives were much slower and were harvested late in December or January, sometimes after the first frost made them black. Spring frost was the big enemy of cherries. The farmers sometimes lit fires in their orchards in an attempt to keep it at bay.

Likewise, growing up into Christ is a slow process, fraught by attendant dangers. The main means of growth is by developing our knowledge of salvation in Christ. That understanding helps us to believe in Him for salvation; trust in Him fosters love for Him. Some more principles will be described to go on from those indicated in the previous chapter. In the following chapters we will talk about maturity and fruitfulness.

How then do believers build up their faith on the foundations laid by biblical teaching?

Progressive development

As well as the growth model taken from agriculture, another striking illustration in the New Testament is taken from personal development. The child becomes an adult, or ought to. In 1 Corinthians 3:1-3 Paul reprimanded the believers at Corinth, who had not grown as they ought to have done:

> I could not address you as spiritual people, but as people of the flesh, as infants in Christ. I fed you with milk, not solid food for you were not ready for it. And even now you are not yet ready, for you are still of the flesh.

A few verses later Paul introduces the image of planting and watering to say that the different ministers of Christ, Peter, Paul, Apollos, etc, do the same work of contributing to growth. Further on in the same chapter he adds another image, that of the foundation and building on it with the right materials in the construction of God's 'temple'. The foundation is Christ, and the building is done by taking on board the apostles' teaching about Him.

In Ephesians 4:13-14, Paul comes back to the same theme and the child-adult development. He talks about:

> building up the body of Christ, until we all attain to the unity of the faith and knowledge of the Son of God, to mature adulthood… so that we may no longer be children…

The way of passing from childhood to maturity is once again by 'faith and knowledge' that grows us into Christ. The apostle Peter, in his first epistle, chapter 2 verse 3, follows Paul's lead:

> Like newborn infants, long for the pure spiritual milk, that by it you may grow up to salvation—if indeed you have tasted that the Lord is good.

And like Paul, Peter adds to the image of newborn babes the idea that believers are 'living stones being built up as a spiritual house' into Christ. Little doubt here either that the 'pure spiritual milk' referred to is the teaching of Christ that builds up believers in such a way that they fit into God's construction with other 'living stones'.

Finally, in Hebrews 5:11-14 to 6:1 the same exhortation appears:

> About this (Jesus' high priestly ministry) we have much to say, and it is hard to explain, since you have become dull of hearing. For though by this time you ought to be teachers, you need someone to teach you again the basic principles of the oracles of God. You need milk, not solid food, for everyone who lives on milk is unskilled in the word of righteousness, since he is a child. But solid food is for the mature, for those who have their powers of discernment trained by constant practice to distinguish good from evil. Therefore let us leave the elementary doctrine of Christ and go on to maturity, not laying again the foundation of repentance …

The apostle goes on in chapter 6 to explain the danger of 'tasting the good word of God' but not growing in Christ. This development to maturity is marked by moving on from milk, 'the basic principles of the oracles of God' to solid food and becoming mature in the 'word of righteousness'.[3] Maturity is a state in which spiritual reflexes that discern what is good and evil have been developed.

In all these texts homely and intimate pictures familiar to the readers are woven together to describe the mysterious principles of growth, in trees, in babies, and in rough-stone building. In each case the means of growth is the Word of God and its teaching. It's as clear as a mountain stream that profiting from biblical teaching should be the prime concern of believers. In fact, if it's not, we leave ourselves open to spiritual stagnation and its attendant dangers—lack of assurance and discernment,

---

3. Hebrews 5:12.

uncertainty and confused ideas, bad habits of unreformed (fleshly) ways, and backsliding—all because we have not connected with the means God has provided for growth.

If that's the case we are like kids who dream of being professional footballers, but who want to get there without practising ball control.

Paul mentors Timothy

This very point is underlined by 2 Timothy 3:15-17. Sometimes it's overlooked because concentrating on the important verse 16 causes us to skip over the reason for its inspiration. If Scripture is inspired it's not with a view to producing an immaculate text that no one can gainsay, as though it had fallen direct from heaven. As God's chosen means of instruction, inspiration records His ongoing dealings with His people in their particular historical situations. Let's recall:

> From childhood you have been acquainted with the sacred writings, which are able to make you wise for salvation through faith in Christ Jesus. All Scripture is breathed out by God and profitable for teaching, for reproof, for correction, and for training in righteousness, that the man of God may be complete, equipped for every good work.

The vital nature of biblical teaching is underlined when the dynamic of the text is set out as follows:

- the foundational principle: knowledge of the sacred Scriptures,
- the substantial principle: profitable teaching, reproof, correction, and training,
- the immediate goal: competence for living,
- the final goal: salvation through faith in Christ.

As Timothy's mentor, Paul encouraged him to become competent in the knowledge that will build up both himself and others. This will be foundational for his preaching of the Word, because he himself has grown mature in it.

Paul is speaking about the knowledge of a body of material—the sacred Scriptures Timothy had known from childhood. They are the source of knowledge which will make him wise for salvation and live a good life in God's sight. They will also arm him against those who are drawn away by their desires or who quit listening to the truth because they can't stomach 'sound teaching'. As a result they succumb to 'myths'. This will happen in the last days preceding the coming of Christ.[4]

Growth in the knowledge of Scripture implies a deepening and a broadening of horizons through personal understanding, because it is 'profitable'. 'Reproof' is the correction of what is wrong by biblical teaching, and 'correction' sets things right. All this is part of 'training', the regular exercise in the gym of good living which tones good spiritual reflexes.

If this is the purpose of Scripture, the practical question is *how* we move on from an elementary understanding of biblical teaching to a well-balanced faith? As we have been given the Scriptures for this purpose, how are we to go about building?

To begin with, young believers are rather like children learning to swim. They begin at the shallow end, practising strokes with difficulty. Then through regular practice they move up to the deep end and go it alone. This, I imagine, is what Paul means by 'training in righteousness'. Moving from the paddling pool to deeper water through spiritual discipline

---

4. 2 Timothy 4:1-4. Most interpreters think that the 'sacred Scriptures' refers to the books of the Old Testament. I am inclined to think, even though it's a minority position, that Paul refers both to the Old and the new canonical writings of the New Testament. For Timothy to be effective in the situation described in 4:1-5, he would need knowledge of apostolic teaching.

and training—right thinking for right living. What then can we do for ourselves, beyond regular practice in Bible reading, prayer, and listening to good exposition of Scripture?

Scripture mentors us

The question of what we can do is not idle speculation. Babies don't think about how to put on kilos, but their mothers have them on the scale every day as soon as they stop putting on weight; trees don't grow self-consciously, but gardeners apply feeder to stimulate growth; houses don't rise from their foundation by magic, architects check that their design is being followed. As Christians we are often exhorted in Scripture to monitor ourselves and to make efforts to take ourselves in hand.

As we dig into Scripture, the main teachings are quite accessible. The average reader can see that the Bible talks about the sovereignty of God, election, creation, providence, Jesus as God and man, new birth and salvation, grace and judgment, suffering, the return of Christ and a thousand other things. However, that doesn't mean that people like or accept these teachings, or that they want to integrate them practically into their way of thinking and living.

A few years ago, a Christian publisher in Switzerland brought out the translation of a book by a respected American pastor with the fine title *The Sovereignty of God.* What a shock for them to receive mail from evangelical Christians who objected to that title! They didn't like the idea of divine sovereignty; they thought it was against human freedom. Where did that attitude come from? Folks who have been reading Scripture for years pass like cats on hot cinders when they come to election. Others balk at the divinity of Christ. This is because a good many people have a pick and mix approach to the teaching of the Bible. Let's just have the chocolate éclairs or the marshmallows and leave the mints out. They are limited tasters. They turn off when subjects they dislike or which raise questions about modern attitudes come up. Nothing is more effective than keeping believers in infancy than this.

If we want to know any sort of growth as believers the 'taster' attitude is counter-productive. It's like putting God in the dock to see if what He says is palatable, rather than letting it challenge us. The only way of dealing with this is by accepting that Scripture as divine revelation is a coherent whole. The believers' calling is to accept it as such. The pick and mix attitude won't wash because it implies we are in the driving seat. We won't let Jesus take the wheel; that betrays a lack of trust in God and a misunderstanding of the greatness of His love for us. This attitude carries over a deep suspicion about God from our unregenerate days. We imagine that God is trying to nuke us in some way, do us out of our freedom, our pleasures or our choices, and to make us puppets. If that's so, we are still enslaved to an anti-God mentality and have not understood that His love for us is like a mother's for her children, wanting only the best for them.

The way of getting over this hump is by humbly deepening our understanding of the big-picture teaching of Scripture and so correcting misunderstandings. This is an aspect of the apostle's 'reproof and correction' process referred to above.

The big picture and its parts

How is it possible to build a big picture of biblical teaching when we read the Bible, attend Bible studies, or listen to preaching? To a good many believers it seems an insurmountable mountain, and one they have little inclination to climb. They never leave base camp.

Birthday and Christmas Lego were a trial of my patience. Fitting together those little pieces that were too small for my fingers was not my idea of festive joy. Being allergic to instructions, my way was to carry on regardless. With Lego that doesn't work, and I was doomed to irate comments from junior.

Building a big-picture vision of the Christian faith is like assembling different pieces of Lego. Biblical teachings are both distinguishable from each other and part of a whole. They come in a pack in the 'sacred writings'. To grow faith in the knowledge of God's grace, we have to put together the individual pieces which, when assembled, form a coherent unity. What the Bible states in its many different propositions gives access to its teachings, and like pieces of Lego, they are designed to go together. From the statements and teachings of Scripture we can build models of what we believe. In some way our efforts resemble the designer model that exists in the mind of God and which He has given us in the form of a historical story in the Scripture print-out. An overview allows us to check that what we believe is faithful to God's revelation. If, as in my Lego experience, we do not follow the maker's model, we soon run into difficulties, which can be corrected by referring again to the Scripture print-out.

The following factors should be taken on board in Bible study:

- the Bible is not a theological textbook which fell from heaven, with its teaching and rules all cut and dried,
- its development is progressive and follows the story of God's salvation, with its relevant teachings more prominent at decisive moments,
- we build a model of biblical teaching by assembling the pieces, respecting how they are different and how they fit together as one picture,

- the outcome is not a repetition of the Bible's words, but presents the teachings of the Bible as a whole,
- our model is a scaled-down version of the big picture existing in God's plan.

Every true believer desires to respect what God has revealed in Scripture. No one who aims at being faithful to divine revelation will play fast and loose with Scripture in building their model. People who study Scripture but do not believe in its authority are sometimes lucid enough to say, 'I can see that the Bible says this and that, but my own take (my truth) on the subject is as follows…'. One such theologian was honest enough to say that the biblical writers believed the Scriptures to be made up of propositional truths, but as a modern person he could not accept that view. One day he asked me the leading question, 'Mr Wells, you don't *really* believe in the inspiration of Scripture as laid out in 2 Timothy 3:16, do you?' The question was pressuring the student to give a negative reply, but I disappointed him.

This critical approach to Scripture might seem very comfortable. It allows you to select in the Bible the elements that fit the modern mentality. Many people say they believe in the person of Christ, but not the Bible. However, this attitude ends up in two uncomfortable outcomes: either you accept that you are adrift on a cruel sea with no island of truth in sight. Why be a Christian at all? Or you seek some dry land in the pick-and-mix attitude that allows you to hold on to something even if you can't accept everything. However, you are sawing the branch you sit on. If you can't trust all of it how can you accept any of it? Both these attitudes present a dilemma because they are inconsistent with faith itself.

At this point someone says, 'But I can't see how to fit any of the teachings of Scripture together. How is it possible?'

Remember, we are talking about knowledge of God and His revelation. It belongs to Him, not us, and for that reason we can expect to find wisdom and coherence in what God says. He speaks 100 per cent through all the biblical writers, even though they are human beings with limitations like ours. So how can we do it?

All the Lego pieces do fit together, in spite of our frustrations: it's just a case of knowing how to go about it. That's what we need to learn as part of 'training in righteousness'. We can expect positive results for three reasons.

Firstly, Scripture bears witness to itself as the Word of God. At this level that means that it shows us the relationship between its various teachings. In their writings the prophets and apostles indicate how the teachings of Scripture are interrelated and how they imply each other. This is particularly so in the way in which the New Testament refers to the Old as fulfilling what was prophesied.

Secondly, the work of the Holy Spirit is to lead Christ's people into the truth and His witness helps us see the truth of Scripture. In Luke 24:44-47 Jesus refers to the Old Testament to enlighten His fellow travellers to the truth about Himself. We can expect the Spirit to open our eyes and see things which of ourselves we could not see naturally.[5]

There is, however, a third way of seeing the big picture, one which is not always fully appreciated in evangelical circles. We are not the first to venture on this path. Our predecessors have faced the problem before us and left wonderful summaries of the biblical faith. We impoverish ourselves by our ignorance of them, whether it be the Nicene creed, the catechisms of Luther

5. Psalm 119:18. In John 16:13 Jesus says that 'when the Spirit of truth comes, he will lead you into all truth', which applies primarily to the disciples-apostles, but through their teaching in a secondary way to believers.

and Calvin or the Heidelberg or Westminster catechisms, and the Reformed or Reformed Baptist (Savoy) Confessions of faith. Knowledge of any one of these is an enormous boon to structuring a growing faith. If you want to tool up as a believer any of these is a good starting point.[6]

One advantage is that these classic texts help us see what we believe as a whole, to have a balance and to avoid majoring in minors. People in many churches lack balance. They ride hobby horses to death by becoming specialists in just one aspect of Christian teaching. In a previous time, it used to be the higher life, or dispensationalism and the return of Christ, now it is more often in the realm of spiritual gifts, or experiences through power encounters, fasting, visualisation, and so on. These believers are sadly doctrinally deformed, having overgrown bodies but heads the size of a pea, and unfortunately they may often be rather gullible.

Getting the big picture

Picture a football weighing 14–16 oz with a circumference of 27–28 inches and inflated to a pressure of 16.0 psi. It is made up of five-sided shapes, called pentagons. The pentagons on the ball all fit together to make a whole. So it is with the teaching of Scripture. It all fits together in seamless unity. Now think of a biblical teaching, for instance sanctification. It stands in relation to *all* the other aspects of Scripture, but it has a close reference to the following: the holiness of God, the work of the Holy Spirit, justification, new birth, the struggle against sin, growth in grace and final perseverance.

Practically, what the Bible says on sanctification stands in relation to everything Scripture teaches, but particularly to

6. For links to historic church documents consult https://reformed.org/historic-confessions/

those doctrines that shine a light on it either by comparison or by contrast. Believers 'grow in grace and the knowledge of the truth' as they think on the teachings of Scripture, how they work together and introduce them into God's way of seeing reality. Meditating on the teaching of Scripture and waiting prayerfully on God sheds light into the nooks and crannies of our life. Light is what promotes growth: 'If we walk in the light as he is in the light we have fellowship with one another, and the blood of Jesus his Son cleanses us from all sin.'[7] This light is life, because God is the fountain of life, and so exposure to light makes us grow.

Like the parts in the engine in a car, all the components of Scripture work together. This is important. You know very well that if the car's spark plugs are dirty, it will affect its running. If it's serious it might reduce your gas mileage or the car will not start at all. Likewise, a deficient doctrine of sanctification will impact other aspects of biblical understanding. For instance, we could get justification and sanctification mixed up and make justification into the dynamic receiving of divine grace. Or we might believe in total sanctification, or perfection, as something possible in this life. This will lead us to water down our understanding of sin so as to claim that being perfectly holy means having no conscious knowledge of sin.

All the teachings of the Bible, whatever we might think of, run together and affect one another. Why? Because God is one, and when He makes Himself known there is a unity in His revelation. That unity finds its echo in our understanding of biblical teaching. So, a healthy understanding of the doctrine of sanctification will relate it to the holiness of God, a recognition of the seriousness of sin, being freed from its power to serve Christ, the struggle that every Christian experiences as being 'at once justified and a sinner' and an understanding of the

7. 1 John 1:7, Psalm 36:9.

progressive growth in grace, leading to perfection which will only be achieved by complete holiness in heaven. Above all it is realistic, because it respects the biblical moorings of the doctrine.

One further point may be made from the football illustration. No one sees the dark side of the moon from the earth, because it faces the other way. In the same way from where you stand, you can't see the other side of a football without spinning it. This reminds us that we never have a complete knowledge of the things of God or a knowledge that is like His. We see what God has revealed, but we have limited vision. We don't see things as God does. We know God because He has revealed His truth to us, but at the same time, He is way beyond us, all-knowing and incomprehensible, which means we cannot 'comprehend' Him and His ways. So we know God as the sovereign and incomprehensible one. Even though we know Him personally, knowing Him is not like knowing other persons. God is the high and holy one, and we must avoid the banana skin of thinking of Him as though He were just a little bigger than us.

So if our knowledge of biblical teaching has a unity, it also has a diversity, because it is always partial knowledge. Four important takeaways follow. Firstly, to know God in a real and true way means being humble about it. Not only do we never know biblical teachings as we ought to (until we reach eternity) because there is always more to learn, but we know *God* and this in itself makes us conscious of our smallness. Secondly, we can never think of ourselves as superior to others, because anything we know depends on God's grace in revealing Himself. If He had not done so, we would have no knowledge of Him at all. Thirdly, if we know God truly by His revelation, we can grow into a fuller knowledge of Him as we build up our grasp of biblical teaching. Finally, to know Him is to know eternal life, since the Word of God abides in us, and we know God who is unchangeable and eternal.[8]

In order to underpin these points we need to branch out a little.

Thinking God's thoughts after Him

We grow as believers because in His great grace almighty God allows us to think *His* thoughts *after* Him. He has given His Word as our 'Rough Guide' of the pilgrimage to heaven. John Bunyan saw this in a brilliant way in his famous book, *The Pilgrim's Progress*. Do we realise how great the privilege is? As we deepen our understanding of God, we grow in our knowledge of Him and in a mysterious way access the same thought world as His. Just as two people living in the same space can become progressively like each other, believers grow together with God through intimacy with His thoughts, what pleases Him, and what brings praise and glory to His name.

Returning to the car illustration. The average car has, I believe, about thirty thousand components. Each part is different, has its own function and dovetails perfectly with the others. Some of them are more important than others. You can still drive if your rear light is not working. The great diversity is part of a unity which gives it meaning. Someone who knows about motors will buy one car, not another because of the quality of its components.

Likewise with the teaching of the Bible. There is a great diversity in what the Bible teaches. Some doctrines are more important to the whole than others. The mighty acts of God in the history of redemption are the central focus for all that the Bible fleshes out. All its doctrinal parts fit together to make a body. God knows perfectly how it all fits together. His

---

8. John 17:3, 1 John 2:12-14.

knowledge of Himself and of all things belonging to His plan is primary.[9]

Our access to these truths, and anything else for that matter, is secondary. It is 'derivative', and depends on God and His revelation. In God there is living, eternal knowledge, a wise and coherent 'system' embracing everything about everything.[10] On the basis of biblical revelation, thinking God's thoughts in tune with Him, we know something about everything included in God's plan. However, we know nothing as God knows it in His divine mind. When Paul speaks about our present knowledge and our future knowledge of God in glory, he says we 'see in a glass darkly'. Our present knowledge is in muted shades. In eternity all that will change to brilliant technicolour.[11]

Understanding about the unity and diversity of God's revelation has practical consequences. It helps us to make something of the fact that there are different theologies, something that troubles many believers. Our knowledge of the teachings of the Bible and the way they fit together gives rise to certain convictions, some of which we will defend with our lives. Take the case of secondary doctrines of the faith. These are non-essentials, unlike biblical teaching on the Trinity, the humanity and divinity of Christ, or the nature of the atonement. Secondary things do not directly affect the outcome of salvation. In the case of baptism, for example, there is a long-standing difference among evangelicals between those who consider credobaptism to be the biblical teaching and those who hold

---

9. The word for God's plan, purpose, or decree in Scripture is in the singular, *prothesis* in Greek.

10. God has 'an existential system of knowledge'. This means God knows everything and all things past, present and future. It means Descartes, the founding philosopher of modern thought, should have said, 'God is, therefore I think' not 'I think therefore I am'.

11. 1 Corinthians 13:12.

to infant baptism.[12] Ultimately the difference depends on how the unity and diversity of the Old and New Testaments and the promise of the covenants are to be understood. It is about how two parts of Scripture fit together. These are tentacular questions. Different interpretations are possible and cannot be resolved simply by quoting the texts that refer directly to baptism.

The rule of thumb to follow with regard to such differences is that of Romans 14:5, concerning the meat offered to idols: 'Each one should be fully convinced in his own mind'. In the preceding verses Paul also warned about being hasty in passing judgment on others, which we are all too prone to do. Differences encourage us to walk by faith and to exercise love for those who think a little differently. The answer will be known later, when we no longer 'see in a glass darkly.'

Two key biblical texts to read together relating to God's knowledge and ours are found in Psalm 139 and 1 Corinthians 2. The Psalm contrasts the all-embracing knowledge of God and, by comparison, our limitations. Verses 1-6 express that God's knowledge is 'too wonderful' for us, 'it is high we cannot attain it.' God knows us, and wherever we are, we can't get away from Him (verses 7-12). God also knows us intimately from the moment of conception through all the days of our life (verses 13-16). The psalmist sums up in verses 17 and 18, by exclaiming:

> How precious to me are your thoughts, O God!
> How vast is the sum of them!
> If I would count them, they are more than the sand.

---

12. Credobaptists believe in only baptising those who make a profession of faith. Those who believe Scripture permits paedobaptism (infant baptism) do not deny adult baptism following conversion. They believe that infants in Christian families constitute an exception as they are raised in a covenantal context.

1 Corinthians 2:6-16 takes a different tack. Rather than contrasting God's knowledge and ours, it sets out how we can know God's thoughts through inspired revelation. Paul sees an opposition between the message of the cross and human wisdom. Christ crucified is a scandal for the Jews. For Greek pagans the cross is a folly because a God who is spirit cannot be revealed, even less crucified, in the flesh. For both these groups the death and resurrection of Christ are the height of senselessness, but for believers they are the power of God. God is wiser than human wisdom. So the message of the dying and rising Christ is salvation for those who believe.[13]

How can the apostle Paul make such an outlandish statement? He sets out his case in the following chapter. It is a 'demonstration of the Spirit and of power', a 'secret wisdom' for the 'mature' that is unknown to the 'rulers of this age'. If they had had any insight 'they would not have crucified the Lord of glory.' He unpacks his thought-line in three steps in verses 9-16:

1. *God has perfectly complete self-understanding.* The Holy Spirit who 'searches the depths of God' has made known these things to Paul. Just as only a person knows their own hidden thoughts, likewise the Holy Spirit searches the deepest thoughts of God and reveals them.

2. *The Holy Spirit is given by the risen Christ.* The words of Paul (and the other apostles with him) are the fruit of them being instructed by the Spirit. They preach as witnesses of Christ; their words are the result of the work of the Spirit.

3. *These things are spiritually understood.* As instruction from the risen Lord, they are opposed to the wisdom of the world. By them Paul states, 'we have the mind of Christ'. The apostles' words are the expression of the mind of Christ Himself through the inspiration of the Holy Spirit.

13. 1 Corinthians 1:26-30.

That any human being might have the 'mind' of Christ is breathtaking. What can it mean? As witnesses of Christ the inspired apostles were given a preview into the 'mystery'. Having the mind of Christ is an insight into God's purposeful plan brought to fruition in the death and resurrection of Christ and the coming of His kingdom and salvation for His people. One day the whole film will be shown. The apostles saw the trailer which is all about Jesus Christ. Scripture leads to Him and from Him. So knowing the mind of Christ gives us knowledge of this great project as Christ Himself understood it, who He was, and what He came into the world to accomplish.

The 'thoughts of God' plumbed by God's Spirit include everything that exists within the circle of God's eternal person and knowledge. There is nothing at all outside it, and the Spirit 'comprehends the thoughts of God.'[14] This hidden mysterious knowledge is disclosed to those to whom God reveals His salvation by His Spirit. In a secondary and derived way, thanks to the Holy Spirit, they can grasp something of God's deep purposes. Scripture gives us the key to God's purposes.

How does this help us to grow in Christ? It is fortifying, because biblical thinking immunises against the virus of worldly wisdom. No matter if unbelievers mock Christianity, those who know Christ will hold fast to salvation in Him against prevailing opinions. God has chosen to reveal things to us and what He has not chosen for us to know, we don't need to know at the moment! There are many things we don't understand, but we don't need to, because what we do know is sure and certain. It's so because it is personal and centred concretely on the grace and truth made known in Jesus Christ. Biblical knowledge does not lead us off into flights of fancy, or pride, but it always leads us concretely to Jesus, 'whom to know

14. 1 Corinthians 2:16.

is life eternal'. He is the key to the big picture of anything else we know in this world.

Is there any greater privilege than being able to think God's thoughts with Him? To sing the song of salvation in tune with His direction? Faith might be like a frail sapling, but with roots deep in Christ and with growth upward in understanding God's ways, it may bend in a gale, but it will not snap.

Recognising the limits

The contrast between God's knowledge and ours is beyond measure, as between the eternal and the temporal, or between what is infinite and the finite. An illustration is the difference between a circle and a hexagon placed within the circle. The circle represents God's infinite, eternal, complete knowledge. It cannot be filled by our knowledge, represented by the hexagon which only touches the circumference at six different points. Our knowledge of the things of God is real and true. Based on God's Word, it joins God's knowledge like the hexagon touches the circle, at the points which the Lord has revealed. However, it is also limited, since everywhere else outside of the six points there is no contact with the circle. God is way beyond us, even more than the illustration suggests since it is not up to picturing the eternal greatness of God.

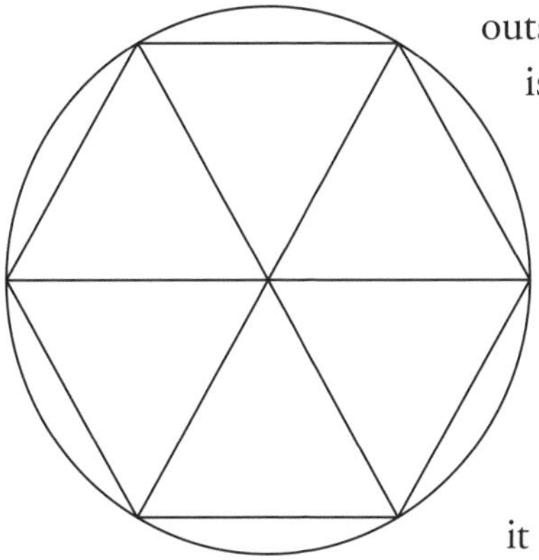

Our understanding of biblical teaching is true, but it is only ever an approximation to God's knowledge. None of us are apt to sit on a brains trust panel conferring with God. That's what Job found out after his trials. In the last chapter of his book he ate a slice of humble pie: 'I have uttered what I did not understand, things too wonderful for me which I did not know… I despise myself and repent in dust and ashes.'[15]

How do we handle what we 'don't understand' and how does it impact Christian growth? Some difficulties in Scripture seem just too big to handle. These questions hold people up and stunt their development. They may be in the vine, to use the image of John 15, but as branches they are hanging off rather than thriving on its life-giving sap. They either become sceptical about God's truth, have doubts about biblical revelation, or circle round the same issue for years like a dog chasing its tail. Even worse, perhaps they are sidetracked into false doctrines (heresies). Not infrequently, when a believer's growth is in neutral or reverse, temptation hits its mark. Moral choices are made contrary to what the Bible teaches, a thing that's easy to do when our hardness of heart and dullness of conscience allows it.

Being fuzzy about what Scripture clearly teaches sullies spiritual life because trust in God is undermined, which in its turn lowers expectations. The practical relegation of the greatness of God is expressed by a refusal to 'let God be God' and to want to have it our way. That's more serious than we think, because we deceive ourselves and directly or indirectly make God a liar.[16]

How can we put a finger on our limitations of knowledge, and flip them from being negative to being a factor that profits growth? Three related considerations that help come to mind: the notion of mystery in Scripture, the kind of information

---

15. Job 40-42, 42:4-6.

16. Romans 3:4, 1 John 1:8.

we can expect from revelation, and the importance of biblical paradoxes.

Firstly, when we talk about the 'mystery' associated with God and His revelation, we need to tread carefully. The divine mystery is not irrational, unreasonable or illogical. God is all wise, which means that He is in no way arbitrary or inconsistent in His person and works, internal or external. Perish the thought that there could be any human arbitrariness in God!

What is beyond our understanding is not beyond God's reason, because our reason is finite and limited. God's isn't in any way. Faith is not against reason, it is simply beyond it. By trusting God, reason finds its resting place in faith, as Charles Spurgeon once remarked. Divine mystery is not in the realm of the impossible, an irrational contradiction of what we consider reasonable. God is perfect and pure reason, and He is perfect wisdom.

This can be illustrated by the biblical teaching about miracles. Miracles may take place when God uses natural means, as with the strong wind parting the Red Sea in the exodus, or they might be beyond us, as when Jesus turned water into wine at Cana. That may be beyond our explanation, but it is possible to make sense of it. If God is the creator of all things He is surely able to put the realities under His control into different configurations. God can move the furniture round in His house, even to the point of making the sun stand still for twenty-four hours. God's power is just that big, there is nothing He cannot do, apart from contradict Himself.

So when the Bible speaks of 'mystery' it is not speaking about the irrationality which for the modern mindset means something inexplicable. In the Bible 'mystery' indicates two things. In Paul's use it often refers to something that was a mystery before Christ appeared. What was previously hidden was revealed in the incarnation. God's plan to unite Jews and

Gentiles in one new creation came to fruition. He drew the curtain back to give a glimpse of the mystery hidden from the birth of time.[17] Paul is amazed that he was called to make known God's plan in Christ for the end of time. This knowledge is from God, not by human wisdom or insight, but through the inspiration that makes known the divine mind.

A variation of the same theme is played in 1 Timothy 3:16:

> Great indeed, we confess, is the mystery of godliness: He was manifested in the flesh, vindicated by the Spirit, seen by angels, proclaimed among the nations, believed on in the world, taken up in glory.

Hidden divinity is revealed in the incarnation of the Son. The accent falls here on the mystery of God Himself who nonetheless appeared in the flesh, and triumphed in the Spirit through the resurrection. We should never balk at the mystery of God, but adore it, and praise Him by confessing the limitations of our creatureliness.

That, not why and how

Secondly, following on from this, because God is mysterious our knowledge of Him is of a certain kind, even when He makes His purposes known. John Calvin repeatedly said that we do not know God in Himself, but only in His saving revelation. We might naturally have an intuition *that God exists*, but we cannot prove it. Discussions about the existence of God are a bit futile. Nor do we know *what God is* in Himself. The being

---

17. Paul refers more than twenty times to the 'mystery of the gospel,' 'the revelation of the mystery,' 'the mystery of God,' 'the mystery of Christ,' 'the mystery of the gospel,' 'the mysteries of the kingdom of heaven,' 'the mystery of the faith'. See Romans 16:25; 1 Corinthians 2:7; Ephesians 3:3-6, 9; Colossians 1:26, etc.

of God is more a question for philosophers than for Christian believers. And they won't get far with 'perfect being' ideas, because only God knows God and perfection is something that doesn't exist in our experience. However, we can know *that God is well disposed toward us*, because of the revelation of the mystery of Christ.

We can put this another way. When we approach God or anything He does in Scripture we are blinkered by our humanity and our sinfulness. We know *that* God is God, *that* He is creator, redeemer, and anything else He reveals Himself to be. However, we do not know the *why* or the *how* behind any of these realities. Recognising this will help avoid a lot of frustrating head bashing and deliver us from useless speculations.

For instance we know *that* God is the creator, but not *why* God created or *how* he created. Neither will any scientist ever know *why* and *how*. They know no more about these questions than anyone else. When they try to formulate a theory to explain the origin of everything they are simply playing at being gods themselves. When we steer clear of the futile *why's* and *how's* we avoid the big ditch of scepticism which leads people to say, 'because we don't understand how God created, He couldn't have done it'.

J.I. Packer argued along similar lines in a famous essay about the atonement, 'What did the cross achieve? The logic of penal substitution.'[18] He warned that evangelicals liquidate the mystery by seeking to explain the why's and wherefores of the biblical teaching of the cross. The goal is not to explain the *how* or the *why*, but to guard *that* Christ died for us in a penal and sacrificial way. The desire to explain things can hide the trap-door of wishing to explain them away. Embracing the *that's* of

18. Cf. https://www.9marks.org/article/what-did-the-cross-achieve-the-logic-of-penal-substitution/

Scripture and steering a wide berth from the *how's* and *why's* is the way to trust in God. It's the path to accepting His unique Lordship and loving Him for it.

When we think about it, biblical revelation does not give us many explanations about anything. It is not explanations we need, but knowledge of what God has done to encourage our trust. It does, however, contain a multitude of *that's,* all that God has done. These are the foundations of the promises of God. God's promises for His people are made on the grounds of what He has already done. They are the most important parts of Scripture for faith and trust, and we should underline them in our Bibles and hold on to them for dear life. Concentrating on God's promises grows wonder, stimulates love and nourishes hope.

Apply this approach, for example, to the question of predestination. Believers often run aground and make shipwreck on this teaching. It is always a question that comes up. Difficulties arise over the *how's* and *why's.* Why did God choose Jack and Jill, not Joe and Jane? How did God make His choice? People tend to reject all idea of predestination because they can't answer the first question. Regarding the second they introduce human free will to explain how God made a reasonable choice. If, however, the apostle Paul had given any credence to either of these questions, he would never have written Romans 9.

That God predestinated some is affirmed throughout Scripture. He chose Abraham not any random pagan, Jacob not Esau, Israel not the nations, the members of Christ's Church and not everyone. The Father even chose the Son to die for us and not some other means! It is in Him that we are chosen. Just count how many 'in Christs' there are in Ephesians 1:4-11. This is why the biblical writers never see predestination as a problem, but always as a subject for praise. They speak about it, not in the language of explanation, but in praise and thankfulness language. Look at how the apostle Paul concludes his comments on the mystery of Israel and predestination in Romans 9-11—with the doxology of Romans 11:36. If we can't do the same we are in trouble!

We will never know *why* or *how*, but we definitely know *that* it is so. In the case of election the fact that there are people who are elect of God in Christ is a challenge to us to make our calling and election sure by faith in Christ.[19]

The same principle applies across the board to all biblical teaching. We are called to trust them as part of trusting in God. Our inclination is to try and explain the *how's* and the *why's* using tortuous logical explanations which may be rationally feasible, but are biblically false. Scripture does not explain the *how's* and *why's,* whether it be with respect to creation, miracles, providence, salvation, the return of Christ, or heaven. Faith should let it rest there, knowing that God never does anything without justice and compassion. Trust Him, and praise Him for His greatness.

Living with paradoxes

Finally, paradoxes. The word 'antinomy' is used to describe a statement that is ultimately contradictory and cannot be reconciled. A 'paradox', on the other hand, is a seemingly contradictory statement which, when examined, may be found to be true. When God reveals Himself in Scripture, there are no antinomies related to His words and deeds, but there are plenty of paradoxes. In fact Scripture is full of them, and we should learn to embrace them and love them, because they are biblical. By respecting these limits we can grow a sound and solid biblical knowledge of God.

---

19. 2 Peter 1:10-11.

Paradox comes into play and is necessary because of the two factors that make biblical revelation what it is. Biblical teaching is neither written on gold pages dropped from heaven, nor is it a copy of some heavenly rules to follow to the letter. On the other hand, it is not an almanac of human wisdom either. When God makes Himself known, He enters created reality, taking on the conditions of human history, culture and language, in order to reveal Himself. The Bible itself is divine *and* human, as God speaks to us in our own language.

This is critical. When a parent plays with a child and uses baby talk there is the paradox of an adult speaking like a child. When God speaks to us, His accommodation involves paradoxes in His communication with us.[20] Everywhere God acts and touches temporal and human reality we find paradoxes that express the presence of the two factors. The divine factor is ultimate, and the human is relative. The two cannot be married together in one coherent explanation, simply because of what they are. Their meeting involves two strands that cannot be joined into one in our limited knowledge. Even in the person of Jesus Christ when the divine and the human natures are united in one person, they are not mixed together or fused into another nature. They are united, but kept distinct in the one divine-human person.[21]

Problems related to biblical teaching often arise by the failure to respect the paradoxes of Scripture and the limits beyond which we cannot venture. These things are apparently contradictory to us; our natural desire is to smooth them out into one coherent explanation. However, when we do this we

20. I am following the lead of Cornelius Van Til and John Frame here.

21. This is the reason for the Chalcedon formula of 451AD stating that the one Jesus Christ is Christ, Son, Lord, Only-begotten, 'recognised in two natures, without confusion, without change, without division, without separation.'

break their balance and end up contradicting what the Bible teaches. By denying one aspect of the biblical paradox, we fall into error. Human reason ends up suppressing the divine-human paradox and replacing it with something that human logic can accept. Our limited way of thinking has lorded it over God's revelation. Once off the biblical straight and narrow acceleration is downhill all the way if the trajectory is not corrected.

The problem with not accepting biblical paradoxes is that we spend years wearing ourselves out with problems that are impossible to solve. Our energy is poured into these apparent contradictions and growth is stunted. Instead of praising God and marvelling at His greatness, we try to think our way out of it. Our reasoning eventually runs the risk of leading us away from the message of Scripture. We become fixated, but not on the glory of God.

Here are some biblical paradoxes we should learn to love, as we meditate upon them. We see more and more how they are complementary, and we come to 'taste and see that the Lord is good.'[22] When we do this God is glorified. Each embraces the whole biblical truth on the question.

- God is one *and* God is three persons
- God is sovereign *and* human beings are free and responsible
- Human beings are free and responsible *and* they are slaves to sin
- The Christian is a free person *and* he is the servant of Jesus Christ
- Jesus is divine *and* human
- Scripture is the Word of God *and* the words of men

---

22. Psalm 34:8. The whole of this psalm teaches us about the blessing of taking refuge in God.

- God is just *and* He justifies sinners
- 'Convert me, Lord *and* I will repent'
- Faith is the gift of God *and* a human response to the gospel
- God gives faith *and* He calls on sinners to repent and believe
- The death of Christ is sufficient for all *and* efficient for believers
- The plan of God includes evil *and* excludes evil
- God is almighty and loving *and* evil is rife in His world
- The cross of Christ reveals both the justice of God *and* the love of God
- God predestines all that comes to pass *and* He accomplishes His will by secondary causes—the free actions of His creatures.

Walking with trust not by sight

If, as believers we walk by faith, receiving the whole truth of Scripture and not just part of it, we will grow in our understanding of the greatness of God and our reliance on Him. This is a liberating experience, because we find true freedom by living out the good news God has made known to us. 'You will know the truth', Jesus says in John 8:32, 'and the truth will set you free.'

If, on the other hand, we push back and try to solve any of the biblical paradoxes by human reason, we will end up subjecting one of their aspects to the other. Invariably the result will limit the power or the wisdom of God or both. Red lights ought to come on when and if this happens, because the God we claim to know is no longer the God of the Bible but some figment of our imagination.

Embracing biblical paradoxes leads to dependence on and trust in God, praise for His greatness, heartfelt prayer, as we lay hold of the *that's* of Scripture and God's promises, love for God, and hope in Him. These attitudes promote intimacy with God as our covenant Lord. Dependence on Him fosters growth in confidence. A sense of wonder develops as the greatness of God impresses itself upon our faith. As believers we will accept that God knows better than we do, and we will gladly submit our reason to His and learn to lean on Him.

This kind of faith will grow up to maturity. We will learn to give God the final word, even when human 'authorities' are against it, because faith is trusting God, most of all when the appearances are contrary. This is what Noah did when he built the ark, or Abraham when he left Ur for an unknown land, what Moses did when he led the people through the sea, or what the apostles did when they obeyed Christ's call to go to all the world with the good news.

Conclusion

Growth takes place when the sap flows up into the branches, buds appear, blossom breaks out, leaves grow and finally the fruit ripens.

Believers are grafted into Christ and His life flows into them through His Spirit. Growth is partaking in Him and His life. The means to flourishing is the knowledge of God and of Christ, with heartfelt trust in what God has revealed. God speaks to us in His Word and in His Son. Knowing what pleases Him, through immersing ourselves in the Word, grows faith and obedience in us. One thing we can be absolutely certain about is that when we trust in the Lord, He will never let us down.[23]

---

23. Psalm 71:1. Echoed in the *Te Deum*, 'O Lord, let thy mercy lighten upon us: as our trust is in thee. O Lord, in thee have I trusted: let me never be confounded.'

QUESTIONS FOR DISCUSSION

1. Why is 'growing' important in the Christian life?
2. Why is it difficult to measure growth?
3. How is it illustrated by the progression from child to adult?
4. What would a childlike faith be like?
5. What would adult faith be like?
6. How does knowledge of the 'big picture' help?
7. How can we think God's thoughts after Him?
8. How does our knowledge line up with God's?
9. Why are biblical paradoxes important? Give examples.
10. What is the difference between the *that's,* the *how's,* and the *why's*?
11. How does all this help you to walk by faith not by sight?

4

MATURITY

Qualities of maturity
The centrality of the mind
Mind renewal
A Christ-like mind
Struggling against sin

Chapter theme: *Maturity is the expression of a life that grows up into Christ. It is the outcome of union with Christ as the qualities that characterised His life transform those who follow His example. The apostle Peter encourages believers to make 'every effort' to attain spiritual maturity. This involves the renewal of the mind. A Christ-like mind makes believers more truly human, in the image of Christ, living as He lived. Maturity is also expressed in the struggle against sin with the help of the Holy Spirit.*

'Our people die well'. So John Wesley is supposed to have replied to one of his cultured despisers.[1] By that he meant that believers have the inner strength to face life's tests, including the biggest one. Where does that come from? It's built by a life of growing into Christ. Believers enjoy their lives to the full and at the same time are serious people, ready for the worst, expected or unexpected. In the words of Hebrews 9:27 the universal sobering reality is: 'it is appointed once to die and after that the judgment'. Are we ready for what's ahead? This is what maturity is ultimately about.

Wesley's 'holy death' is unimaginable for most people. Bucket lists are about places to visit, not how they want their inner character to be changed. In a day of leisure, pleasure and influencers, maturity is strictly for fuddy-duddies and kill-joys. Who thinks about being mature, or aspiring to it? That's about getting old, right, and we all want to be younger. When feelings and experiences are at a premium we don't hear much about maturity in Christian teaching either.

However, as the outcome of growth in Christ, maturity is central to the message of the New Testament. It features qualities desirable for all believers. These should be first on our list of things to become, since they define how we react when faced with the real issues of life. If we are mature in Christ, we will find the inner strength to stand up to the challenges, which will happen to each one of us. The danger of thinking that what we have in this life is all there is, as people around us who have no faith in Christ do, is that we go to pieces when difficulties arise or unexpected disaster strikes. Which is perhaps why we hear so much today about mental health issues. It's also why believers aspire to something different. So what do you know about the qualities that promote maturity?

---

1. Wesley was influenced by his reading of Jeremy Taylor's book, *The Rule and Exercises of Holy Dying* (1651).

Quality street

As we mentioned previously, the apostle Peter's exhortation to believers in his second epistle (3:18), written a short time before his martyrdom, was to 'Grow in the grace and knowledge of our Lord and Saviour Jesus Christ.' In this final letter he speaks about the knowledge of grace from personal experience. It is the way to peace, the evidence of God's power, and the remedy to being ineffective. Moreover, the increasing recognition of who Christ is insures against false teaching, and assures of Christ's return in glory to establish a new creation.[2] Revealed truth is important for believers who without it would 'lose their stability' under the influence of the 'error of lawless people.'[3]

But that is not all it does. In 2 Peter chapter 1 the apostle refers several times to the factors that promote maturity. He addresses his readers directly about spiritual progress in a mini sermon with three points:

1. God has given believers what they need to become spiritually mature (3-4);
2. They must actively work for maturity (5-9);
3. This is the way to a welcome into God's eternal kingdom (10-11).

The second point focuses on what we must do to mature in Christ. The rather unusual expression in Greek in verse 10, to 'make every effort' to secure salvation, encourages us to put all our energy into it.[4] The payback for this investment, as verse 8 says, is an increase in maturity in Christ. God works in the lives of believers in difficult situations.

---

2. 2 Peter 1:2-3, 5-6, 8, 12, 20; 2:20-21; 3:2-3, 17-18.

3. 2 Peter 3:17.

4. Which is rather like 'work out your own salvation with fear and trembling' in Philippians 2:12.

Peter did not use the Greek word 'quality' as our translations do, but referred to the 'things', or kinds of attitude, that show spiritual grit. He is not talking about some namby-pamby niceness, but about practical attitudes, because 'when the going gets tough, the tough get going'.

2 Peter 1:5-9 is an encouragement to practice the things that seal the calling and election of believers and assures them that they will not fall. Eight of these qualities are in italics below (emphasis added):

> Make every effort to supplement your *faith* with *virtue*, and virtue with *knowledge*, and knowledge with *self-control*, and self-control with *steadfastness*, and steadfastness with *godliness*, and godliness with *brotherly affection*, and brotherly affection with *love*. For if these qualities are yours and are increasing, they keep you from being ineffective and unfruitful in the knowledge of our Lord Jesus Christ.

Although preachers sometimes do so, it is not quite right to take these verses as a progression with each of the qualities representing a step up. Peter is not using 'elevator logic' but a form of repetitive speaking his readers understood. A better way of looking at it is to picture a wheel with the 'knowledge of Jesus Christ' as the hub, the 'qualities' being the spokes supporting maturity, which is the rim of the wheel. Maturity or lack of it in believers is where the rubber hits the road as they navigate the bumps and potholes in the tarmac of life.

So what can be said about the qualities the apostle selected to contribute to Christian maturity? How can we own them? What are they and how do they work?

Peter names eight to aim for. It's not an exhaustive list, because more such qualities can be found elsewhere in the

New Testament.[5] What we do have here is an exemplary selection representative of a life aspiring for maturity. One way of understanding it is to consider what each of these qualities represents and to think of the opposites that would have described the lifestyle of the pagans of Peter's day. So we can build two identikit lifestyles, one of a maturing believer, and the other of a pagan following the day's trends. A third picture can be added of today's paganism which is also centred on 'virtues', signalled by minorities who are vocal in their advocacy of 'progress'. Both these forms of paganism, ancient and modern, are in stark contrast to a Christian mentality (see page 116).

What is surprising about Peter's list is that he uses some of the buzzwords of Greek virtue philosophy to pinpoint Christian qualities. 'Self-control', 'godliness', and 'knowledge' were foundational Greek 'virtues'. They marked out the aspirations that put the élite 'good life' above the common people. Noble though these particular virtues were, even the most honest pagans did not live up to them and fell foul to the counter-productive attitudes common in the cruel ancient world. The modern world with its woke virtues reboots the old pagan mindset. It also presents virtues, but it's a cruel world where nonconformity to the crowd provokes hatred. Look at the way J.K. Rowling has been cancelled for her so called 'TERF' feminist views. Disciples of Christ, then and now, take their distance, and aspire to a better way.

Not law but grace

In Peter's list of 'virtues' he turns the ideals of the Greek élite on their head by starting off with 'faith' and finishing with

5. For other lists of qualities see Romans 5:1-5, Galatians 5:22-23, Ephesians 4:31-32, Philippians 4:8-9, Colossians 3:12-16, James 3:17-18.

1. Qualities that contribute to maturity in Christ	2. Counter-productive pagan values of Peter's time	3. Virtue signalling in modern paganism
Faith in God (pistis)	Pagan superstitions (all is one)	No God. Crowd identity rules
Goodness (virtue, aretē)	The 'good life'	Social justice virtues
Knowledge (gnōsis)	Myths, gods and goddesses	What's trending now
Self-control (enkrateia)	Desires	My truth
Steadfastness (hupomonē)	Inconsistency	Group platforms and action
Godliness (eusebeia)	Christian belief is a folly	To each their own belief
Brotherly affection (philadelphia)	Indifference to the fate of others	Promotion of group values
Love (agapē)	Interest in one's own social class	Self-love and interest

'love'.[6] That sets the tone for Christian living in the whole of life. For Greek thinkers faith was considered to be in cahoots with superstition, something related to feelings and emotions like fear, rather than a quality based on reason or facts. That was not Peter's take.

2 Peter 1:14-21 underlines that faith is rooted in the eye-witness testimony of God's action—something seen, heard, known and felt as real. It has firm roots in reality and the power of God's objective acts, in contrast with the 'cleverly devised myths' of pagan knowledge (*gnosis*). Believers seek to live in a way that is faithful to reality. The love Peter finishes this section with is *agape,* the love of total self-giving for another. It's neither convivial friendship nor eros love, but the love of 1 Corinthians 13, also described by Jesus in John 15:13: 'Greater love (*agape*) has no one than this, that someone lay down his life for his friends'. When you have faith, it's so real that love follows and together they kick-start faithfulness to Christ.

Qualities for Christian maturity begin with faith and lead on to love for God and one's fellows. Faith is a firm assurance of and faithfulness to what God has revealed in creation and salvation. Love is not being in awe of beauty and perfection, but a self-giving, trusting commitment. Between faith and love stand the qualities of goodness (virtue), knowledge (wisdom), self-control (moderation), steadfastness (perseverance), holiness (godliness) and brotherly affection (looking out for others). Together they make an identikit picture of Christian living, or to put it better, they image the true humanity that Peter saw on the mount of transfiguration.[7] Believers shine out those qualities because they are in Christ and joined with Him in one Spirit who is at work in them.

---

6. Faith leading to love, is the order found in Romans 5:1-5 and 1 Corinthians 13.

7. 2 Peter 1:14-21 and Matthew 17:1-9.

Reading this repertoire of ideal qualities might discourage struggling believers when they look at themselves in the cold light of day. But it's not a 'to do' check list. Two things are to be remembered:

1. This list is *not law but gospel.* Jesus fulfilled the law for us by His active obedience and in His passive obedience to death itself. When we are one with Him growth in these qualities is growth into Him, closeness to Him in the way He lived on earth. So Christian virtues are not like Greek virtues or like woke virtue signalling, which are forms of *self-salvation by works.* While they are totally different, both of these embody religions of self-realisation and self-esteem. Believers on the contrary know they have no merit, and live by faith.
2. Secondly, and because of this, when faith focuses on Jesus, and when love for Him is the goal, we will grow up into maturity in Him by fellowship with Him, as *His* grace towards us shapes our lives. Believers live by a love that is Christ's love.

This is truly knowing God, walking in the light by faith and love. It is productive of the qualities Peter refers to. Paul puts it more dramatically when he speaks about maturity, but like his fellow apostle, he is referring to believers' efforts to strive for the same things. In Philippians 3:13-14 he states: 'Forgetting what lies behind and straining forward to what lies ahead, I press on toward the goal for the prize of the upward call of God in Christ Jesus.' With great humility Paul affirms that he does not consider himself to have reached the maturity this higher calling implies. We can take it that we too have a long way to go and a lot of effort to put in. The jackpot question is: how do we invest so as to practically strive for maturity in Christ? How can we press forward with an eye on these qualities?

The answer is by living a life centred on Jesus. Four perspectives will help to keep the goal of maturity in view: The key role of the mind, its renewal, Christ as our ideal model of humanity, and the believer's struggle with sin. So let's focus on them now.

1. Your mind matters

The first perspective of a life centred on Christ indicates how the *mind* promotes maturity in the life of Christ's followers. The mind is a central factor in the Christian's view of what we are and how we function as *persons*. This is why the Reformers and the Puritans often spoke of the 'primacy of the intellect'. What were they getting at?

We might not immediately locate our spiritual problems or our progress towards maturity in our mind, but rather in our emotions that tell us we feel 'good', or in the will to do the right thing. However, I think that would be a mistake; the biblical emphasis on 'grace and knowledge' as the mainstays of the renewed life alerts us to this. However, because it's not obvious to everyone, let's explain.

Yesterday I saw several ships sailing in and out of the river Mersey. So let's imagine a boat, and make a comparison with human persons so as to see the importance of our mind in how we function. A ship has a hull, a bridge, a rudder and engines, all of which make up its 'shipness'. Comparing those features with our humanness, as persons we have a body, a mind, a heart, emotions and will. Together they make us the people we are. The body is like the hull of the ship, the mind is the bridge, the heart sets our fundamental direction, whereas our feelings and will are like a ship's motors. Feeling and will are the dynamic duo that drive us forward into action. They are motivators; we will not freely do anything without the inclination to do it.

Like the bridge of the boat, the mind is the *decisional* centre where the situation of the vessel is seen, the radar and the compass are consulted. From the bridge the captain powers or cuts the motors, and shifts the direction by the rudder. The understanding is the nerve centre, evaluating and judging everything, it takes on board what we feel and want, where we are going, and what our body is telling us. It is vital as the information collector of our person, and it makes decisions. Even if our 'motors' power us to act, they need information to make decisions and conscience to evaluate them before and after we enact them.

These personal factors function as a unit. Biblical revelation also tells us that we have something deeper, unknown to scientific observation, that tends to reduce the mind to a collection of cells—a heart that is a symbol of what makes us tick as persons. The heart is *directional* and it sets our destination. So we are exhorted to 'guard our heart' since the 'issues of life', are determined by it.[8] Our heart is personal and relational and is the point at which our personal inclinations unite so that we do things 'with all our heart', with 'a deceitful or wicked heart', with 'a heart that's pure and true' or with a 'new heart'. If we really want something we 'put our heart in it', but when our team goes 3-0 down, we will 'lose heart'. The heart indicates the final destination human beings choose, our destiny, in a personal and spiritual sense.

The heart is a spiritual organ and as such it has a dual aspect. In biblical revelation it has a covenantal or bonding function, in relation primarily to God and also to others.[9] What we are invisibly, deep inside, sets our direction, which is why we act

8. Proverbs 4:23. Jesus likens the heart to our 'treasure', Matthew 6:21.

9. The Christian philosopher Herman Dooyeweerd says that the heart is the transcendent unity of the person related to God. Cf. *In the Twilight of Western Thought*, (Philadelphia: Presbyterian and Reformed, 1960).

with 'a hardened heart' towards God and our fellows. The word of God came repeatedly to Pharaoh in Exodus 7-12, but the Egyptian king hardened his heart against the Lord, and made light of Moses' request. Pharaoh understood very well what God was ordering, but he didn't like it at all, and set his will against it. He would not let the children of Israel go, and that sealed his fate.

In addition, the heart unifies mind, body and will. This is because the heart is *in* the mind, *in* the will and the emotions, and *in* the body. The heart is our unity of purpose as persons, and sets our course to an ultimate goal. A 'wholeness' is provided by the heart. Because of our fundamental attitude of heart we are either running toward God, or running away from Him. So David prayed in Psalm 51:10-12:

> Create in me a clean *heart* O God,
> and renew a right *spirit* in me.
> Cast me not away from your presence,
> and take not your Holy Spirit from me.
> Restore to me the joy of your salvation,
> and uphold me with a willing *spirit.* (emphasis added)

A cleansed heart is a right mind (the spirit here), one that is willing and joyful because of salvation. So we see the movement:

> When God changes the *heart* a person is transformed,
> The *heart* changes the *mind* of the person,
> The *mind* has a new *will* to please God,
> *Heart, mind and will* impact the *emotions.*

This illustrates the right order for approaching the question of the mind's role in developing maturity. 'It doesn't interest me', 'I'm not motivated', 'It grabs me', 'How good is that?' always jump to the front of the queue. But they are secondary and counterproductive. Gut reactions affect Christian life and worship with creeping anti-intellectualism, because the 'mind' is reduced to something that belongs only to 'intellectuals'. The danger of this was underlined many years ago by John Stott:

> But the fact that man's mind is fallen is no excuse for a retreat from thought to emotion, for the emotional of man's nature is equally fallen. Indeed, sin has more dangerous effects on our faculty of feeling than our faculty of thinking, because our opinions are more easily checked and regulated by revealed truth than our experiences.[10]

That hits the nail on the head. It is more difficult for the mind to escape from reality than it is for feelings. Sadly many Christians don't get this, because they are dictated to by their emotions and fail to engage their minds with faith. Worse, because feelings rule, they disobey things clearly taught by Scripture because their feelings rebel against them. In this way, many unwittingly follow the world; their mentality is neither renewed nor differentiated from their feelings. This prevents them from facing up to things in the Bible that seem difficult, for example, the doctrine of hell, that election includes some, not others, why Jesus is the only Saviour of the world, why being a good person is not sufficient for God, or even why sexual choices are important.

Like the human will, the mind exists in a fourfold state: created, fallen, renewed and glorified. If our mind is important how does it become a renewed mind?

We no longer know what the created mind would have been like before the fall, because sin has put paid to it, and the glorified mind, restored fully in the likeness of Christ after the bodily resurrection, is still future.

---

10. John Stott, *Your Mind Matters,* (IVP, 1973) (2007), p. 16.

Today, like God's image in man, if the human mind has wonderful capacities, it is fallen because it no longer receives the things of God. Why?—Because naturally it is a closed mind, self-centred and self-absorbed. The apostle Paul uses the expression 'old or natural man' to express what the mind of a fallen person is like. 1 Corinthians 2:14 states: 'The natural (*psychikos*) person does not accept the things of the Spirit of God, for they are folly to him, and he is not able to understand (know) them because they are spiritually discerned.'

The sinful mind is an expression of a heart turned away from God. When we are looking one way we can't see behind us as we haven't got eyes in the back of our heads. So the heart turned away from God shows itself in a mind turned away from God and spiritual realities. Its state is darkness. Those who 'live according to the flesh set their minds on the things of the flesh … [and] to set the mind on the things of the flesh is death.'[11]

However, the human mind, though fallen, is still God-designed, and personal remainders of the dignity and the nobility of the created state are seen all around us. We still aspire to goodness, justice and truth, we can still distinguish beauty from ugliness, and right from wrong. All human inventions are double-sided; we are capable of the best and worst.

The fallen nature impacts the whole person: the heart, the mind and will, and mental states have physical consequences too. It is wrong to locate the seat of the fall and sinfulness in our physical nature. When Paul speaks about the 'natural person' the problems he lists concern the *mind*: egoism, ambition, pride, covetousness, desire, or self-destructiveness. The great theologians have located the propensity to sin and evil in the mind: Augustine in pride, Calvin in idolatry and

11. Romans 8:5-6.

failure to worship the Lord, Karl Barth in human indolence toward God.

So what is the solution? Christian faith knows only one answer. No moral or spiritual improvements or progress will make human nature whole again; like the decay in a tooth, the rot in an apple, or a valve stuck in an engine, we never improve, neither in our own sight if we are realistic, and even less in God's. The only solution is a change of heart and the transformation of the spiritual discernment, the mind with its mental capacities.

2. Mind renewal

The second perspective of a life centred on Christ is the biblical notion of the renewal of the mind, about which the apostle Paul speaks primarily in Romans 12:1-2, using the Greek word 'transfiguration' (*metamorphosis*):

> I appeal to you therefore, brothers, by the mercies of God, to present your bodies as a living sacrifice, holy and acceptable to God, which is your spiritual worship.
>
> Do not be conformed to this world, but be transformed by the renewal of your mind, that by testing you may discern what is the will of God, what is good, and acceptable and perfect.

This text is a turning point in the epistle to the Romans. The apostle's intention is to show that salvation in Christ for all nations is manifested in the fulfilment of God's covenant, renewed one final time. Salvation integrates Jews and Gentiles into a people united in Christ and set apart or sanctified in Him. Renewal is expressed concretely in these verses.

The first verse draws on the Old Testament context; the second refers to the Greek thought-world. As the new covenant goes beyond the old, the second verse goes further than the first. The sacrifice is accomplished once and for all in Christ and the offering of believers is now not a material one, but spiritual or reasonable (*logikos*). They no longer present animal sacrifices, but their own 'bodies', meaning their whole persons or selves, as 'living sacrifices'. Believers go counter to the accepted narratives around them; they take their distance from the non-biblical mindset of the present day by the transformation of the intelligence (*nous*).

At this point the apostle looks back in his epistle to the first two chapters and to the sin that alienates from God. Romans 6:13 is a key to Romans 12:1. In contrast to the state of sin, believers are encouraged:

> Do not present your members to sin as instruments for unrighteousness, but present yourselves to God as those who have been brought from death to life, and your members to God as instruments for righteousness.

Looking ahead to Romans 15:8-16, the apostle contemplates that Christ became the servant of all, Gentiles as well as Jews, so that the Gentiles might hope in him and might be a pleasing offering, sanctified by the Holy Spirit.

This new situation is not a political platform. It comes into effect through the conversion of the moral conscience, the intelligence, transforming the personhood of believers. Humanity renewed in Christ, destined for the new creation, is contrasted with the old. The whole person, including 'the body', so depreciated in the Greek world, is united to Christ by the transformation of the mind through the Holy Spirit.

How does this take place? The word 'metamorphosis', used half a dozen times in the Bible, gives a pointer. The face of Moses was transformed by the glory of God on Mount Sinai, where the law was given. Moses covered his face because the children of Israel couldn't stand the brightness. Jesus was transfigured on the mountain with Moses, Elijah and His three disciples, a foretaste before His suffering of His future glory as the Son of God, risen from the dead. In the presence of the risen Christ, believers 'with their faces unveiled, reflect like a mirror the glory of the Lord... transformed into the same image, from glory to glory, as by the Lord, the Spirit.'[12] Jesus is all that Moses was, the mediator, the shepherd of His people, the one who gives the new law, performs miracles and leads to the promised land. But He is even more glorious! As the 'beloved Son of God' and Lord He renews the people of God in a complete and final way. So to Him alone God's people must listen.

In Romans 12:2, as spokesman of the living Christ, Paul the apostle gives two parallel exhortations for his readers. If the first is negative, 'do not be conformed', the second is positive, 'be transformed'. The apostle is a realist, and he knows that sin sucks us down like quicksand, even when we are regenerated and united to Christ. Ethical transformation to maturity only takes place when we live self-consciously in Christ, looking constantly to the Risen One. The Spirit changes us according to Christ's image as a result of this face to face encounter. Sanctification results as the dynamic of revolutionary change in our conscious minds. The imprint of the image of Jesus transforms our mentality and reboots our entire life.

It is not surprising then that the epistle to the Romans ends with the names of thirty unknown Christians, who live the new life by sharing in Paul's ministry to bring salvation to their fellow Romans. What God has done for the world calls for a reaction from His people and we, the readers, are included:

---

12. For the transfiguration of Jesus, Matthew 17:1-8 and parallels in Mark and Luke, and 2 Corinthians 3:18 for Paul's reference to it. See also Colossians 3:10.

the offering of the self in willing service to the Lord and the transformation of the mentality are the way to maturity.

To sum up. The mind is renewed by the direct action of the Holy Spirit that believers receive when united to the living Christ by faith. This enlightening of the mind goes hand in hand with a change of heart, because a person's life is changed. The heart and mind impact the actions of the will and the feelings in communion with Jesus, and so reach out in the bodily realm. Sanctification is the growth of ethical newness of life into Christ's likeness; maturity in Him is the goal.

In the well-known movie, *The Bourne Identity*, Jason Bourne becomes a secret agent by committing himself to the Treadstone programme. He commits to the mission and takes on a new identity. The Christian life is not 'falling in love with Jesus'. It's more covenanting by faith to love and obey Jesus, putting ourselves on the line and committing willingly to His programme. God, who justifies us in Christ, also sanctifies us by faith in Him. The progress of sanctification to maturity is the work of the Holy Spirit. It brings with it the assurance that we are really and truly reconciled to God. Commitment is life and peace in service to Christ, as we learn to trust and develop a Christ-like mind.

But can more be said concretely about the workings of a renewed mind? How do we experience it? Four practical attitudes come into play in a Christ-like mind.

3. A Christ-like mind

The third perspective of a life centred on Christ concerns the Lord Jesus Himself and the way He lived His life on earth demonstrate what true humanity is. Jesus is the role model for believers' maturity.

Did Jesus react on the spur of the moment to the challenges of life, with salvation the outcome? No, He was a man on a mission. The Greek word *dei* meaning 'must' is used many times in the Gospels to suggest the 'oughtness' of Jesus' ministry.[13] He *must* fulfil the Scripture, He *must* suffer and die, He *must* work the works of the one who sent Him. His programme, both in deed and word, was set out for Him by God the Father and He executed it to the letter. This is the witness of Jesus Himself concerning His work, in particular in the Gospel of John:

> The Son can do nothing of his own accord, but only what he sees the Father doing. For whatever the Father does, the Son does likewise.
>
> The works that the Father has given me to accomplish, the very works that I am doing, bear witness about me that the Father has sent me.
>
> For I have come down from heaven, not to do my own will but the will of him who sent me.
>
> For I have not spoken on my own authority, but the Father who sent me has himself given me a commandment—what to say and what to speak.[14]

Jesus is the one who was sent. He listened to the Father, received His message from Him, spoke and enacted it, and so obeyed the Father's will. This was complete and total obedience. Jesus gave the disciples the prayer, 'Your will be done on earth as in heaven' because that is what He Himself was doing. When we follow Jesus, we do God's will by becoming like Him. Jesus learned from the Father, being one with God, called the twelve

---

13. Used over a hundred times in the New Testament. See any Bible concordance.

14. John 5:19-20, 36, 6:38, 12:49. This is prophesied in the servant songs of Isaiah, cf. Isaiah 50:4-8.

to become His disciples, then we as Christian believers become disciples and follow the path of Jesus.

Evangelicals are sometimes reticent about speaking of Jesus as our model out of fear of reducing His work to a simple example of a good life. However, that danger should not lead us to forget that Jesus' life does show us the model of humanity as it should be, because Jesus is the second Adam.[15] In His human nature He models how we should be and shows that the goal of knowing God is concretised in the wisdom of obedience to Him. The mind of Christ is not that of a great scientist, an entertainer, a teacher, or a psychiatrist. He shows perfectly what obedience to God entails. He lived out the model for true humanity in—

- trust and love for God,
- obedience to God through perfect service,
- true caring, compassion and love for others, even to giving Himself for them,
- courage to follow through His calling to the end,
- being without sin, either mental or bodily,
- unsullied emotions, including joy and peace in suffering, shedding tears for His friends, lamenting over the lostness of sinners, righteous anger, etc.

Perhaps you know some grifters in your work, your social activities, or your family. Jesus in His humanity was the opposite of all you despise in them. Here is a person you can really admire! He lived out His life as no one else could, never thinking of Himself. He submitted to God's life-project and followed it through to its conclusion, along the tightrope of perfect freedom and true responsibility. He was broken down by

15. Romans 5:12-20, 1 Corinthians 15:22.

untold suffering, but never stopped hoping in God's salvation. When He died, His assurance was that God, according to the promises of Scripture, would deliver and justify Him. But humanly, like us, He had to believe it.

So Jesus is the role model for how to speak, to live, and what to be in submissive service to God. The more we are in His presence, the more we know Him, the more His image will reflect in us. But how does this happen, in such a way that the human qualities of Jesus rub off onto us? Is that possible? It seems to be something totally beyond our reach, but is it…?

We follow the model of Jesus by 'possessing Him'. To be justified and sanctified, says John Calvin, we must first possess Christ.[16] When this is real, it's not we who are striving for better, but Jesus who is acting in us, who is united to us by the Holy Spirit. The way to true humanity is through a renewed heart via a renewed mind expressed in the virtues we spoke of earlier. 'Possessing Christ' changes our direction and grows out into our whole personality. The new person is constantly being renewed even though the physical body declines with the years.

Obviously, someone can know the gospel, understand the message and have no personal interest in it. Something miraculous must happen. The Spirit changes the heart and then the mind is enlightened, as when lights are switched on in a dark room. The Holy Spirit illuminates the truth of the written Word in a way the unbeliever cannot know. The ministry of the Spirit is to seal the truth of God in hearts and minds as we possess Christ for salvation. This is 'putting on' Jesus Christ, clothing oneself in Him, in order to walk in the light of newness of life.[17]

---

16. John Calvin, *Institutes of the Christian Religion*, III.16.1, III.11.1. In Galatians 1.16 the apostle Paul states that Christ revealed Himself 'in me'. By receiving the same gospel we receive and possess Christ.

17. Romans 13:14, Galatians 3:27, Colossians 3:10, 12.

4. The ongoing struggle against sin

The fourth perspective of a life centred on Christ is that just as Jesus fought against sin and overcame it, so those who are His disciples take up the same struggle. Having the mind of Christ by the work of the Holy Spirit is the stand-out feature of the new life of believers. This makes us different from those around us with whom we share a common social identity and similar feelings. It means we struggle with sin.

Much of the struggle against sin takes place in our conscious mind. It is important not to let our minds become obsessed by the rubbish that the media pour into them. A young believer told me recently that she catches herself thinking thoughts she shouldn't and she has to pull herself up by saying, 'Stop, that's not who I am!'

To be like Jesus is to be submissive and obedient to God, as He was in His humanity. Believers become like Him, not fully or perfectly, but more and more, really and truly, little by little, by 'putting off' the old nature, or 'putting it to death.'[18] The unfashionable notions of submission to God, obedience to His Word and self-giving in sacrifice are the lost keys to a happy life. How do they come to living expression?

A neglected teaching among Christians today is that of the struggle against sin in progressive sanctification. This struggle takes place in the Christian mind, which is a feature of the renewed heart. John Stott again says:

> Perhaps the current mood (cultivated in some Christian groups) of anti-intellectualism begins now to be seen as the serious evil it is. It is not true piety at all but part of the fashion of the world and therefore a form of worldliness. To denigrate the mind is to undermine foundational Christian doctrines. Has God created us rational beings, and shall we deny our

18. Colossians 3:5.

> humanity which he has given us? Has God spoken to us and shall we not listen to his words? Has God renewed our mind through Christ, and shall we not think with it? Is God going to judge us by his Word, and shall we not be wise and build our house upon this rock?[19]

The biggest obstacles to growth in maturity are our will and our emotions that struggle against what we know to be true. We 'do not want to' engage in combat to bring 'all into submission to Christ' because we do not 'feel like it'. How can we come out on top in this inner struggle? Two ways exist by which believers win out.

Firstly, we must be realistic about how Scripture presents our human makeup. Martin Luther was correct in using a Latin phrase to describe the tension we experience as Christians. He said we are *'simul justus et peccator'*, meaning at the same time justified and sinners.[20] When we understand this, we recognise that:

- Our heart has to be submitted to the Lordship of God and recognise that this is our situation,
- Our mind, our Christian understanding, must take distance from our feelings,
- Our knowledge of what is true and right must tell our feelings to 'shut up', as in the case of the friend referred to above.

So we do not allow our irrational and sinful desires, fears, hopes, or other feelings to obsess our Christian mind. If we

19. Stott, *Your Mind Matters*, p. 26.

20. In 1535 in his commentary on Galatians 5:16 Luther wrote, 'We are partly sinners and partly righteous. Yet our righteousness is more abundant than our sin, because the righteousness of Christ, our propitiator, vastly surpasses the sin of the entire world.' The apostle Paul expressed this tension in Romans 7:21-24.

are following Christ we cannot live thoughtlessly in exactly the same way as the world. This is easy to do, because our uncontrolled feelings lead us into things that are agreeable for a moment but end up in destructive outcomes. What the French poet said of romantic love—'the pleasure of love lasts only a moment, the heartache of love lasts a lifetime'—is very true of sin as well. 'Solid joys and lasting treasure none but Zion's children know' said the old hymn-writer.[21]

Secondly, Scripture gives precise instructions about what we should *do* about our sinful inclinations. A key passage is Romans 8:12-14:

> So then, brothers, we are debtors, not to the flesh, to live according to the flesh. For if you live according to the flesh you will die, but if by the Spirit you put to death the deeds of the body, you will live. For all who are led by the Spirit of God are sons of God.

This 'mortification of the flesh' as John Owen called it, is the principle means, often neglected, of making progress to maturity in the Christian life; other newfangled 'methods' prove unproductive, because they are not biblical. To what does Paul exhort us?

He warns believers of living heedlessly 'according to the flesh' in the broadest sense. Following the way of the world leads physically and spiritually to death. A Christian cannot live like this. We must consciously renounce the life habits of our past, and we can, because we are no longer under their power, as verses 8-9 state. This is a must for every Christian. Blindly following the world's thinking and ways will only undermine assurance of salvation, 'if at least the Spirit of God dwells in us'.

---

21. John Newton in his hymn 'Glorious things of thee are spoken' (1779).

Paul states furthermore that if 'Christ is in us, the body is dead because of sin'. This means that the dominion of sin, of the flesh, has been broken. The reality of this becomes evident by killing off 'the actions of the body', illegitimate physical desires, in all areas of life. The former dictator of our life has been dethroned and dealt with on the cross. It's up to believers, in reliance on the help of the Holy Spirit, to gradually demolish the remnants and influences of the old life and its harmful hold. Christ is the new king: His reign and justice must spread little by little everywhere—'If Christ is in you, although the the body is dead because of sin, the Spirit is life because of righteousness' (8:10).

Given the magnitude of this task, how can we not be discouraged? But we must not, because we are not alone! We have to act through the Spirit of life, who unites us to Christ. The Spirit attacks the 'mildew' of sin and allows the vines to bear mature grapes. How can this be? The Holy Spirit is:

- *the gift* of the living Christ. The fight against sin is carried out with the Spirit's assistance, under the sign of Christ's victory, which constantly sends us back to the source of salvation accomplished for us on the cross;
- *the power* of Jesus Christ, who lives with us and in us. The Spirit of holiness raises us to walk in newness of life with the Lord Jesus. Unity with the Lord is spiritually real, living, and even physical (because our bodies belong to Him);
- *continually effective*, because wrestling with sin with His help finally results in success. We are not always full of praise, and we cannot claim to have reached perfection. If sin is with us in our bodily dispositions until the end of our days, the Spirit helps us to throttle it little by little and so to remove its power.

In this fight to the last we are exhorted to hope for the future liberation as children of God. Is there any better incentive to persevere?

Maybe you think: I know it, but I don't manage to do it! The fear of failure dogs me and holds me back. Take courage, brother or sister, no one does it fully, but everyone can set out on this road. Here are some practical hints as to how we can go about it:

1. Practice honest self-evaluation: are there habitual sins in our life that develop into a cancer, because we have never truly wanted to uproot them? Anger, self-absorption, pride, jealousy, sensuality, lies, etc.? Do we often succumb to them? Then resolve, before God, to uproot them to resist their lure … and pray.

2. Be realistic about the havoc that particular sins wreak. Analyse how they hurt you, how they affect your peace and joy, how they bring you into conflict against the 'better you' and also with others. Remember that complacency about indulged sin is both hurtful to your Lord and it saddens the Holy Spirit.[22] Are you, in the words of Dr Martyn Lloyd-Jones, 'spiritually depressed'?[23] Do you need help to work through your problem?

3. Determine in which specific situations you are most prone to succumb to temptation to sin. Avoid them if possible. If this is not the case, prepare spiritually for battle and try to control your thoughts by focusing them on the Lord's greatness, His blessings and the great truths of salvation in Christ. In other words, and in concrete terms, as soon as a small breach appears in the dike of your defences, plug it

22. Ephesians 4:30-32.

23. D. Martyn Lloyd-Jones, *Spiritual Depression: Its Causes and Its Cure* was first published in 1959.

immediately, before a flood occurs. Try to find support and encouragement from prayer and from someone close.

4. Finally, be aware that these useful human attitudes in and of themselves are not enough. Turn your eyes to the cross. It is there that Jesus conquered sin and set His resurrection power in action.[24] Look at what He has done for you and at what cost! Be thankful. Pray. Confess your past sins. Ask the Lord to give you His power to prevent repeats. And believe that He can and will!

Paul concludes his exhortation with a promise. If you do this, 'you will live'—in Christ, in depth, now and forever. And don't forget the old saying, only dead fish float downstream.

A successful struggle against sin is a leading factor in sanctification, because continuing sin in believers makes the Holy Spirit cringe. When they take the conflict with remaining sin seriously in their lives, they make strides forward. As Paul says in Romans 6:22: 'Now that you have been set free from sin and have become slaves to God, the fruit you get leads to sanctification.'

Conclusion

In 1 Corinthians 6 when the apostle Paul deals with practical problems in the church at Corinth, he questions his readers six times (in verses 2, 3, 9, 15, 16, 19), 'Don't you *know* this, don't you *know* that'? No appeal is made either to their will or their feelings, 'don't you feel that?' but he focuses on what Christians believe because of what they know to be true:

> Do you not know the the unrighteous will not inherit the kingdom of God? Do not be deceived: neither the sexually

24. Ephesians 1:19-20.

> immoral, nor idolaters, nor adulterers, nor those who practice homosexuality, nor thieves, nor the greedy, nor drunkards, nor revilers, nor swindlers will inherit the kingdom of God. And such were some of you. But you were washed, you were sanctified, you were justified in the name of the Lord Jesus Christ and by the Spirit of our God.

Paul is not claiming that believers are better than others, simply that they are different: their minds have been changed, they have come to see things in a different light, and the Holy Spirit gives them power to change.

Again in his second letter to the Corinthians Paul appeals to their convictions about things believers know. Beyond knowing things, conviction of the truth is what transforms our way of living. So the apostle says in chapter 5:11 and 14:

> Knowing the fear of the Lord, we persuade others...For the love of Christ controls us, because we are convinced of this: that one has died for all ...

Knowledge with conviction is the sign of maturity that a gospel world-view brings. We will have to see how this works out in greater detail in our final chapter about bearing fruit.

QUESTIONS FOR DISCUSSION

1. Why do you think Peter spoke about virtues?
2. What is their significance?
3. Describe how our world is anti-christian in its values.
4. What is the importance of the mind?
5. Discuss the two quotes from John Stott in this chapter.
6. What is the importance of Romans 12:1-2?

7. How is the Lord Jesus a model for believers?
8. What is a mind like Christ?
9. What is the mortification of sin?
10. Discuss the four ways of dealing with ongoing sin.

5

FRUITFULNESS

The believer's experience
King harvest will surely come
Fruit to the glory of God
Fruit by living in hope
A top-down perspective

Chapter theme: *Fruitfulness is the end point of the growth process. The New Testament attributes it to the work of the Holy Spirit. It is a foretaste of the new creation which is the real outcome of the work of Christ who is the 'first fruits of those risen from the dead'. Real fruit is harvested in eternity. It grows now by living in hope of the future, because God is a God of hope who delivers from the slavery of sin and futility. Hope encourages believers to see things critically from God's top-down perspective.*

Figs are delicious and delicate fruit, best picked right off the tree and eaten on the spot, skin and all. Near where we lived in the south of France a smallholder used to set up by the road and sell figs he called 'honey drops'. I've never tasted anything like them. A few days before being ripe figs are hard, soon afterwards they are squishy, but on the day there's nothing to beat them.

The believer's experience

In His mysterious purposes God is preparing believers for 'ripeness', which means eternal enjoyment in His presence. That is our goal, when our fruitfulness will be ripe in complete union with the risen Christ. Before that time comes, we are not yet ready. However, in this life we have some foretastes of the goodness that lies ahead, because the fruit is ripening. Augustine commented that by His grace God gives us the good works that we do, in such a way that He is working in us: 'even those good works of ours, which are recompensed with eternal life, belong to the grace of God, because of what is said by the Lord Jesus: "Without me you can do nothing".'[1] That is true, and consequently we look to Jesus and to the work of His Holy Sprit, not to ourselves, in order to be fruitful.

Fruit is the outcome of the growth process. Well seeded plants put down roots, grow out and up, bud, then blossom into flower. Finally fruit appears and matures until harvest time. Spiritual fruit is the outcome of gradual growth to maturity in Christ. Fruit forced in the greenhouse is tasteless by comparison with naturally ripened fruit. Similarly, in the spiritual realm method induced growth ('how to'...) is often artificial. It is not the real McCoy, often described by experiences which are too full blown to be taken seriously. Miracles that don't last,

1. Augustine, *Of Grace and Free Will*, chapter 8.

prophecies that don't come true, or stories from hearsay that can't be checked out. People soon lose their appetite for them.

For the best result, fruit should be picked at the right moment. Prematurely it is bitter and hard. This reminds us that life is tough at times. Believers are not always shiny, happy people; there are difficult episodes in life marked by discouragements, dashed hopes, or burn-out. Often we are disappointed with ourselves, and at times with others who betray us, but Jesus will never be a letdown and even less will He let us go. Grace will help us to the other side of the swamp of despond. Above all, the worm of sin will not finally destroy our fruit. Christ's death is the pesticide that dealt with sin once for all at the cross.

In one of his early sermons, Jonathan Edwards, the Great Awakening revival preacher, laid out three points about the experience of believers:

- bad things will finally work for good according to God's purposes;
- in Christ what we have gained cannot be taken away from us;
- the best things are yet to come in the future.

These points speak of fruit in Christ. The 'best things yet to come' describes the fact that the real fruitfulness of believers in Christ is not in this world but in the life eternal, the final resting point in Christ. Then we will reach full stature as children of God in a new creation.[2]

Seeing this is important. It will deliver us from the creeping desire for perfection, which is a trap for us all. There is no perfect fully-grown fruit in this life. We should be satisfied if a

2. Jonathan Edwards, 'Christian happiness', preached when he was eighteen. Cf. Colossians 1:28.

'little progress' has been made toward the goal, as John Calvin liked to say.

King harvest will surely come

We are tempted when talking about fruitfulness to jump right into a discussion about what people call the fruits of the Spirit in the New Testament. That would be to forget that even those fruits, real though they may be, belong to the present age, when we are still waiting for something even better. So it is important to put them into context, and see what their implications are for the Christian life, not forgetting that they are part of the expectation of the final harvest.

That the final harvest is in heaven Jesus made clear in His explanation of the parable of the good seed and the weeds in Matthew 13:37-43:

> Jesus answered, The one who sows the good seed is the Son of Man. The field is the world, and the good seed is the sons of the kingdom. The weeds are the sons of the evil one, and the enemy who sowed them is the devil. The harvest is the end of the age, and the reapers are angels. Just as the weeds are gathered and burned with fire, so will it be at the end of the age. The Son of Man will send his angels, and they will gather out of his kingdom all causes of sin and all law-breakers, and throw them into the fiery furnace. In that place there will be weeping and gnashing of teeth. Then the righteous will shine like the sun in the kingdom of their Father.

The point of Jesus' parable is that in this world good seed and weeds grow together. Although this describes the tensions and struggles of this life for the believer's growth and the frustrating work of the adversary, God's purposes ripen fast to the inevitable end. Then the causes of opposition will be rooted out of our lives. Fruit will be gathered in the sunlit harvest of God's kingdom. Nothing will ultimately prevent the fruitfulness of the children of the kingdom. King harvest will surely come!

This bigger picture is also hinted at by the New Testament expression 'firstfruits', which underlines that any fruit we produce now belongs to the harvest that Jesus began with His resurrection from the dead. In Israel the firstfruits were presented according to the law of Moses in recognition that the land and all its produce were gifts from God to be returned to Him. The fruit of the soil and prepared foods were brought to the priest as God's representative, and a part of them was offered as a sacrifice on the altar.[3] This is the background for the apostle Paul calling Jesus 'the firstfruits of them that are asleep' in 1 Corinthians 15:20-23. Following His sacrifice on the cross, Jesus presented Himself to God as the first to rise from the dead with the promise of a full harvest, the resurrection of all His people at the last day. Following this pattern, those who belong to Jesus are called 'a kind of firstfruit of his creatures', and the 'firstfruits of the Spirit'.[4] They are a token of the harvest to come, the resurrection of the body and deliverance from sin, death and the devil.

In Revelation 22:2 the tree of life reappears at the end of the story of salvation. It reminds us that our sin against God is the consequence of our forebears having taken the fruit of the tree of the knowledge of good and evil. This tree is literal but it has a symbolic meaning. I imagine that its fruit was like durian fruit in Indonesia, which the locals say tastes like heaven but smells like hell.[5] Eating the forbidden fruit stinks the place out. Corruption, death and the judgment of exclusion from God's

3. Exodus 23:16, 19, Leviticus 23:9-14, Deuteronomy 26:1-11.

4. James 1:18, Romans 8:23, 1 Corinthians 16:15, Revelation 14:1-5.

5. A hotel where I stayed in Indonesia had the rule in the rooms: 'Make no soup in kettle, no durian fruit, no immorality in rooms'!

presence followed hard on the heels of the sin of disobedience. Human experience had now become a mixture of good and bad. Access to the other tree, the tree of life, was forfeited at the dawn of time.[6] But at the end, the tree of life in the heavenly city has twelve kinds of fruit, it yields fruit each month and has 'leaves for the healing of the nations'. Again we have a literal tree with a wonderful symbolic meaning. There is healing from sin, which is permanently renewed for ever, and for all the people of God. It comes from the Lamb who sits upon the throne and the river of life that issues from Him.[7]

Looking at the beginning and the end of the biblical story helps us understand why the notion of fruitfulness is so important in the teaching of Jesus and the apostle Paul, and also for what is expected of us.

Central to Jesus' message, using the pictures of trees and their fruit, is the idea that a fruitless tree wastes space. This theme comes from the Old Testament prophecies.[8] Matthew Henry comments on Ezekiel 15:2-3 that 'those who are not fruitful to the glory of God's grace will be fuel to the fire of his wrath.' Fruitless fig trees, olive trees and vines are useless. They are cursed and replaced by good trees that bear fruit. The unfruitfulness of Israel is not the end of the story. Isaiah 27:2-6 states that Israel will once again become a pleasant vineyard: 'In days to come Jacob shall take root, Israel shall blossom and put forth shoots and fill the whole world with fruit.' This does not refer to the national Israel today or in the future, but to the drama of Jesus' time. After telling parables in Matthew 21 and quoting from Psalm 118:22-23 about the stone the builders

6. Genesis 2:9 and 3:4-5, 22-24.

7. If the tree of life is the sacrament of the first covenant, in the end the tree is the sacrament of eternal forgiveness, symbolised at present by the bread and wine of the Lord's supper.

8. Hosea 9:10, 10:1, Ezekiel 19:10-14.

rejected becoming the cornerstone, Jesus says some terrible words in verse 43: 'Therefore I tell you, the kingdom of God will be taken away from you and given to a people producing its fruits.'

For this very reason, Jesus in John 15:4-5 exhorts the disciples who will become the foundation of God's new covenant people to persevere in Him:

> Abide in me , and I in you. As the branch cannot bear fruit by itself, unless it abides in the vine, neither can you, unless you abide in me. I am the vine: you are the branches. Whoever abides in me and I in him, he it is that bears much fruit, for apart from me you can do nothing.

Jesus instructs His followers to abide *together* in Him. Their unity in His truth is essential to growth, and He will grow in them when together they proclaim His truth. This is how the vine will 'fill the whole world with its fruit.'[9]

The apostle Paul picks up the ball at this point. In a very real sense all fruit in Christians is the gift of Jesus and His work in us, not of our efforts. When He rose to heavenly glory, He did so through the power of the Holy Spirit. He became the one who 'owns' the Spirit that He gives from heaven to produce fruit in the lives of those who belong to Him.[10] The gospel bears fruit and grows, and Paul prays for believers' spiritual wisdom and understanding. Then they will 'walk in a manner worthy of the Lord, fully pleasing him, bearing fruit in every good work and increasing in the knowledge of God.' His earnest desire is that His spiritual children be 'filled with the fruit of

9. Hosea 14:4-7.

10. 2 Corinthians 3:17-18. What Paul means by 'the Lord is the Spirit' is that now Jesus is present with His people by the Holy Spirit.

righteousness that comes through Jesus Christ to the glory and praise of God.'[11]

Paul has three basic things to say about spiritual fruit. Here they are:

1. As in the teaching of Jesus and the Old Testament, he takes up the contrast between the unfruitful works of darkness, the fruit of the flesh or the 'natural man', and the fruit of the light and holiness of life. The first is bitter fruit to death and the second is sweet fruit to God.[12] The contrast is so stark that you don't have to be a saint to see it, although you do have to be a saint to see it!

2. Paul contrasts the fruit of the Spirit and the gifts of the Spirit, such as prophecy, speaking in tongues, etc. Every Christian bears the fruit of the Spirit, but the gifts of the Spirit are given to certain people in order to serve others.[13] This is the opposite to what we might think. The gifts are not for us, but bestowed for the good of others in the body of Christ; the fruit certainly is for us because it refers to our personal growth (even though others will benefit indirectly from the fruit we bear). To put it another way: the gifts do not grow us, and we do not necessarily become mature because of them, but we certainly do by the fruit.

3. The fruit of the Spirit is one, like a single bunch of grapes, with nine fruits in one cluster:

---

11. Colossians 1:6, 10 and Philippians 1:8-11.

12. Ephesians 5:9-11, Romans 6:20-22, Philippians 1:11, 22 and Romans 7:4-5.

13. In Galatians 5:22-23 the 'fruit of the Spirit' indicates nine attributes of bearing fruit: love, joy, peace, patience, kindness, goodness, faithfulness, gentleness and self-control. There is said to be either seven, nine or sixteen gifts of the Spirit, according to different interpretations. See 1 Corinthians 12:1-11.

> The fruit of the Spirit is love, joy, peace, patience, kindness, goodness, faithfulness, gentleness, self-control… those who belong to Christ Jesus have crucified the flesh with its passions and desires.[14]

The final phrase of this list is important. Sometimes the 'gifts' are the reason for passions and desires, dividing the church, as they did at Corinth. That's because they are taken to be badges of merit; people's self-esteem and self-identity hangs on them. The lurking problem is pride, as the apostle infers in 1 Corinthians 13:1-5. The danger is that all you love is need—the need to have that gift. Love for others in Christ as the fruit of His Spirit will not lead down that blind alley, because it's humble self-abasement.

Finally, in a cluster of grapes, they all look alike. The nine fruits Paul lists resemble each other because they all come from the Holy Spirit who unites us to the Lord Jesus. When this is the case, these qualities begin to grow in us, as the dispositional attitudes Jesus Himself showed during His life on earth. They describe the way He lived and died. When we belong to Him, what empowered His life moulds the way we live. Growing into Christ, we bear His fruit in our lives through the Holy Spirit who unites us to Him. If love tops the list, as in 1 Corinthians 13, it is because love infuses all the others.

So do I bear the fruit of the Spirit? is the same question as do I show Christ-like attitudes in my life? Does my disposition bear witness to love, joy, peace, patience, kindness, goodness, faithfulness, gentleness, self-control? And that is the same question as, 'Am I living my life in Christ in the here and now?' That's a bottom of the line question. It shines a light in our paltry little lives. Of course we will be uneasy, as few of us can honestly reply in the affirmative. What should we do? Well,

14. Galatians 5:22-24, compare with Colossians 3:12-17.

there are two answers to that. The first is to get nearer to the Lord Jesus with all the will we have. The second is that if we find this difficult to do, as is the case for most of us, we are to wait on the Lord. We ask, seek and knock, until it's opened to us, as Jesus teaches in Matthew 7:7-12. This tallies with James 1:5: 'If any one lacks wisdom, let him ask God, who gives generously to all without reproach, and it will be given him. But let him ask in faith, with no doubting…'

The reason we don't bear fruit as we would like is often because we do not earnestly seek it.

Fruit to the glory of God

Wisdom, knowledge and bearing fruit are signs of lives lived to the glory of God. That is the main purpose of our lives on earth, and it will be our occupation in heaven. If we are to bear fruit now, the best way to do this is to focus on God and His glory. What does this mean and how can we do it?

The first question and answer of the Westminster Larger Catechism stands out:

> Q. 1. What is the chief and highest end of man?
> A. Man's chief and highest end is to glorify God, and fully to enjoy him for ever.[15]

There are three pointers here that contribute to understanding how believers bear fruit to the glory of God.

1 The reason for this question and answer

The first five questions in the Catechism are about God and man, revelation and Scripture. They are foundational

15. Romans 11:36, 1 Corinthians 10:31, Psalm 73:24-28, John 17:21-23.

attitudes for exercising the Christian faith as a whole. Get the foundations wrong and the whole building will be out of kilter. The Catechism doesn't start with God alone or man alone, but with God *and* humanity.

We cannot speak of God in Himself or humanity in itself, but only of their relation, one with another, as Scripture reveals it. This is the heart of the Protestant reformation.[16] Faith is concerned neither with the nature of things, whether God exists or not, nor with proofs for His existence, but with God and man in relation—how God is disposed to us and the knowledge that flows from it. It is not the being, existence, or even the sovereignty of God that are in focus. Glorifying God starts with a personal relationship. This makes all the difference.

Four consequences follow on from this:

- God is the ultimate reason for creation and human beings. Like it or not, we have ultimately to do with God, and to give account to Him;
- God is simultaneously above all (we glorify Him) and close to us (we enjoy Him);
- What makes the world go round is God's saving love for a lost world;
- The perspective is covenantal. God is a covenanting God who calls His people and unites them to glorify His name.

So this question indicates that as human beings we can never find true meaning in our lives without God. We find it in covenant with Him. How then are we to glorify God?

16. Witness Martin Luther's theology of the cross and the first chapter of Calvin's *Institutes.*

2 What does it mean to glorify God? Why is it man's purpose?

The answer to the first question sets the tone for the answer to the second.

We are to glorify God because it's what God Himself does. God's glory is eternal and personal. God is a Trinity of persons who love and glorify each other eternally. According to Scripture God glorifies Himself in three complementary ways:

- God is self-glorifying

God is the only one who can be self-glorifying, because God alone is God and He alone can live up to what it is to be glorious. What annoys us about human self-glorification is that when others puff themselves up by self-advancement they are soon found out. By contrast, the three persons of the Trinity are all glorious, and this is reflected in their love one for another. The Father loves the Son, the Son loves the Father and the Spirit is all-divine love. The Son is the radiance of the glory of the Father.[17]

- God glorifies Himself in creation

The glory of God overflows into His creation. The act of creation is a work of Trinitarian love, and it is all 'very good'. Psalm 8 speaks about the remarkable greatness of God and also about His nearness. While His name is majestic in all the earth and He sets His glory above the heavens, yet He also witnesses through the 'mouths of babes and infants'.

- God glorifies Himself in salvation

17. John 17:1, 4-5 and 17:22-23, Hebrews 1:3.

Psalm 145 speaks of the greatness of the glory of God and underlines His works of salvation, the 'awesome deeds' that He has done:

> The LORD is gracious and merciful, slow to anger and abounding in steadfast love.
>
> The LORD is good to all, and his mercy is over all that he has made.
>
> All your works shall give thanks to you, O LORD, and all your saints shall bless you![18]

God's glory in salvation overflows into the new creation, since His kingdom is an everlasting kingdom. God glorifies Himself by announcing salvation in the new creation.

God is therefore man's purpose, or chief end, in life. As an intelligent covenant creature, man is drawn into glorifying God. Why are we here? To glorify God, for no other reason. Our purpose is to glorify God, which is our chief calling among others, and if we can do that we will be fruitful. Two things need saying about how we can focus on this:

- We glorify God because God has commanded it

No human being can make demands on others to love them. It's what every dictator wants, which is why they go on walkabouts and have photo opportunities with cuddly infants. But they end up generating fear and hate, not love. With God it's different. In many places in Scripture God commands us to delight in Him, to magnify His name, to give thanks, and above all to love Him. Just as God alone can legitimately glorify Himself, God alone can command love for Himself. Why? Because love is something that He knows deeply and perfectly, and it's already

18. Psalm 145:8-13, Revelation 4:9-11 and 15:3-4.

complete in Him. God is perfect love and for that reason He is the standard for all other loves, and is to be glorified as such. 'Love the Lord your God with all your heart, soul and mind' is a covenant command. In His love and majesty God associates us with Himself as we love Him and give Him glory. But there is also a subsidiary reason for loving God.

- We glorify God because it does us good

Glorifying God is our reasonable response to what God is, just as breathing is part of living. We can even say it's our duty or covenant response. We are created in God's image, and, in loving the godhead, we actually find ourselves. God commands us to love Him because our mission as human beings is to glorify Him. When we do, we not only enjoy it, which is no doubt something that seems impossible or even alienating to other people but lose nothing and gain everything, because loving God is pure pleasure.

3 How are we fully to enjoy God?

As believers none of us fully enjoys God, and we can often feel guilty about it. We are not joyful enough; our love for God is lukewarm, not on fire. That's because none of us really glorifies God in a whole-of-life way. We get bogged down by present concerns, which are legitimate in themselves, and then stuff takes over our lives. However, glorifying God is not a law, but a gospel call (or duty, as used to be said) arising from a vision of the wonder of God and the greatness of His love. When we see the glory of God, the consequence for us is to enjoy, delight, and take pleasure in the beauty of it all. We glorify God *and* enjoy Him.[19] It's like opening your eyes on awaking to the bright

---

19. Glorify *and* enjoy, not glorify God *by* enjoying Him as John Piper suggests (*Desiring God*, 1986). The enjoyment is a *consequence* of glorifying God, not the *instrument* for glorifying Him.

morning sun after a week of rain: it's pure delight. Pleasure in God starts in this life and is complete in eternity, where it will be whole and unadulterated. If we can make a little start here we will find satisfaction in the fruit of enjoyment.

Many Christians think that glorifying God is about getting together for a praise music hoedown. However, there is more to it than that. Praising and glorifying God is about more than a sing-along, it's an all of life disposition. I imagine that glorifying God in eternity might be about fulfilling a new heavenly cultural mandate. A variety of holy activities that glorify God in transformed service will praise Him and satisfy us. The ministry we will have as restored creatures will be as multifaceted as our renewed humanity, serving God in the length and breadth of the renewed universe.

As we await the glorious return of Christ there are four basic ways believers can glorify God and enjoy Him here and now:

- By confessing God as Lord and lifting up His name

The doxology of Romans 11:36 provides the model. We worship the Lord recognising that '*From* him and *through* him and *to* him are all things. To him be the glory' (emphasis added). God is glorified when we confess that everything we see ultimately comes *from* Him as His creation. It's all *through* Him as providence upholds and unfolds all things, and everything is *to* Him, like great rivers flow to the sea, which describes the glorious end in His new creation of righteousness and justice.

- By receiving His Word seriously and following its instruction

Psalm 73 speaks about a person oppressed by the way the arrogant and wicked prosper, whose 'eyes swell out through fatness'. But his despair only lasts until he goes into God's presence and sees what end awaits these monsters. For Christians suffering persecution and martyrdom under the boot of the world's tyrants, what can be said? Verses 23-26 of the Psalm give an answer:

> Nevertheless I am continually with you; you hold me with your right hand.
> You guide me with your counsel, and afterward you will receive me to glory.
> Whom have I in heaven but you? And there is nothing on earth that I desire besides you.
> My flesh and my heart may fail, but God is the strength of my heart and my portion for ever.

It's reassuring to know that God never lets tyrants enjoy their ill-gained power for too long.

- Worship with God's people glorifies God's salvation

Church services are boring for many modern people. This, I believe, is because our worship has lost a sense of God's presence. It does not start with the invocation, God calling together His people to meet them. To begin a worship service with a flat 'good morning' is to forget the wonderful truth that this meeting is like nothing else, because *God invites us into His presence*, which is the meaning of the word 'church' (*ekklēsia*). When we know that God is calling us to meet *Him,* to worship and hear His law and gospel, to receive His forgiveness, this is the important event of the week. Much more so than any other event. So we understand the feeling of the psalmist, 'I was glad when they said to me let us go to the house of the Lord'.[20]

- Praising God through the right use of His creation

Glorifying God does not begin at the gates of the Temple. What happens there is the passing from the secular to the sacred, but that is a very limited view. What happens every minute of every

20. Psalms 122:1, 42, 43, 87.

day and in every inch of creation belongs to God. 'The earth is the Lord's and everything in it' says Psalm 24:1. Just as the heavens belong to the Lord God and declare His glory in Psalm 19:1-6, so the created earth is no less His. To be able to worship God in His world and receive His blessing requires 'clean hands and a pure heart' as Psalm 24:3-5 states. The way has been opened for us by the risen Lord Jesus. Paul quotes Psalm 24:1 just before 1 Corinthians 10:31 where he states: 'whether we eat or drink, or whatever we do, do all to the glory of God.' In this context, Paul's teaching on the question of the meat offered to idols is that everything belongs to the Lord, and therefore we can do everything, including eating and drinking, to His glory. But he cautions that we should also respect the feelings of others and avoid giving offence to those who might have a troubled conscience in the way we act as believers. There are no limits to praising God's glory in His creation, but for some things love for our neighbour will rein in our freedom out of respect for their conscience.[21]

4 Attitudes that encourage the enjoyment of God

Human beings as created before the fall must have known how to glorify and enjoy fellowship with God. They waited for Him with joy. However, they would also have had to learn how to do it in two ways. They had to learn how to relate as man and woman and to follow the 'cultural mandate' by working and keeping the garden sanctuary. Both areas of life implied a development and a learning process. After the fall into sin, glorifying and enjoying God was eclipsed by fear. Glorifying

---

21. Christian liberty exists in those things which are considered things indifferent or *adiaphora,* because there is no direct command about them one way or the other in God's Word.

God was no longer something to bear fruit. Even when we are regenerate and growing in Christ, glorifying God does not come naturally.

We have to relearn how to glorify and enjoy God. We need to work at it through spiritual exercise. It's like drinking coffee. Most young people don't like it to begin with, but later they get into coffee culture and instant is definitely uncool. The move is made up to Americano, but real coffee enthusiasts (like me) will not take anything other than a double espresso, no sugar and certainly none of those syrup flavourings.

There are three formative attitudes for learning to delight in God:

- Taking time to admire just how great God is

We do this by savouring His greatness particularly as revealed in Christ, in His divinity and humanity. As the Puritans used to say, when we 'think great thoughts of Jesus' other things pale to insignificance. Think, for instance, of how the Lord Jesus was hated without cause throughout His ministry, yet He reacted to this in a pure and sinless way.

- By delighting in God's glory

The fear of the Lord is the beginning of wisdom. This 'fear' is being struck by the fact that God is overwhelmingly awesome. God is the Lord and we feel very small, as in 'what is man that you are mindful of him'? But God is also our Saviour, and the intimacy of His promises and perfect love tempers fear. We are drawn out of ourselves to worship Him in prayer. You don't go to the local canal to be struck by a breathtaking view. You go to the Grand Canyon. There you will be knocked over by the stupendous sight, and you might even be scared to go near the edge. Likewise, we enjoy God and take pleasure as we approach Him and behold His wonder and beauty, but at the same time we are overcome by the prospect of glory. Look at the case of Isaiah in chapter 6 of his prophecy. Or John in the first chapter of Revelation. Like all the saints of the Bible when they meet God they fall on their faces, but then intimacy overcomes their fear as God is reassuring and merciful. So we appreciate the glory of the Lord and take pleasure in what we see.

- By thankfulness to God

All that God gives us we learn to receive with thankfulness and joy: happiness, hardship and suffering alike. A hospital bed may become the place from which the faithfulness of Christ shines out. We 'count it all joy', even when we are put to the test for the sake of the gospel, as James 1:2 says. Why so? Because this testing makes for steadfastness, which when it is complete makes not just for simple belief, but for an authentic faith, one that is so firm that it takes life's hard knocks.

John Piper sums up:

> God is most glorified in us when we are most satisfied in Him. Christ is magnified as a glorious treasure when He becomes an unrivalled pleasure.[22]

Fruit by living in hope

The Bible teaches us two basic things that promote being fruitful: what we are to believe about God, His ways and works, and what we are to do to mirror that belief.[23] Faith is not complete without a practical expression. But how is that possible? Christians know how to obey what the Bible teaches and how to make it fruitful in their lives. They do so by a

---

22. John Piper, *The Dangerous Duty of Delight*, Multnomah, Colorado Springs, 21, 27. Piper has much to teach us on the subject (even if I don't like the expression 'Christian hedonism'). The Grand Canyon illustration is his.

23. *Westminster Larger Catechism*, Q 5.

positive and lively hope in God. The portrait gallery of the Old Testament faithful in Hebrews demonstrates that believers continue to trust in God, and look to eternity, contrary to all appearances and discouragements. So Moses 'considered the reproach of Christ greater wealth than the treasures of Egypt, for he was looking to the reward.'[24]

1 God's promises produce fruit

The Bible does not speak about God in the third person singular or make abstract statements about Him. God speaks in the first person singular in a personal 'I and you' relationship. He tells us what He has done in His great acts. God acts in creation, in deliverance, and gives *promises*. So the God of the Bible asks us to believe in Him as the God of hope, who will demonstrate His faithfulness in the future. As we look to Him, hope bears fruit in our lives, saving them from emptiness, discouragement and despair.

Hope is present right from the start of the biblical story. It is hardwired into the human constitution by God's promise of life. Not only does the creation week have a future-oriented perspective, leading to rest with God, but the human psyche, created in the image of God, has eternity programmed into it. From the beginning, God's covenantal dealings with man point to future completion. Biblical hope has two aspects: it is hope for deliverance and hope that overcomes emptiness.

2 The God of deliverance

When sin excludes man from God's sanctuary, human life becomes enslavement ending in death. Anxiety, fear, and emptiness kick in. God intervenes and delivers through exodus

24. Hebrews 11:24-28.

promising new beginnings. The exodus theme grounds the hope of God's people from Abraham onward. We think often of the exodus from the slavery of Egypt which is the most striking model.[25] But there are repeated 'exoduses' in the Bible: Abraham is called out from the paganism of Mesopotamia and receives promises for the future, for His descendants and for the whole world;

- The exodus from Egypt and the pilgrimage to God's sanctuary in the promised land is the fulfilment of the hope given to Abraham;
- Later, a further return from judgment in Babylon repeats the Egyptian exodus and fulfils the biblical prophecies. It gathers God's people together again into a kingdom, with a rebuilt temple, to wait for the promised Messiah;
- When Jesus the Messiah finally comes, by His death and resurrection those who believe in Him are raised by faith to new life and follow Him in triumphant procession of His people. He leads them into the new creation.[26]

So the entire biblical narrative circles around hope of liberation from the bondage of sin and the entry into God's promised land. As believers we become part of an exodus people, delivered from sin, raised with Christ and awaiting the final victory He will bring. This is the Christian hope. Life is a pilgrimage with a destination, as John Bunyan so aptly saw in his *Pilgrim's Progress*.

---

25. See chapter 1 on Jesus and God's new people.
26. Hebrews 11:8, 27, Luke 9:28-36, Ephesians 4:8.

3 Freedom from emptiness

Romans 4:18-22 presents the experience of Abraham as a model for faith.

> Against all hope, Abraham in hope believed and so became the father of many nations… he did not waver through unbelief regarding the promise of God, but was strengthened in his faith and gave glory to God, being fully persuaded that God had power to do what he had promised. This is why it was credited to him as righteousness' (NIV).

Abraham's 'hope against hope' looked to God in the absence of human means, when all indicated the contrary. Abraham models the fact that when all seems hopeless and there is no reason for believing apart from God's promise, faith takes over.

There are many great moments in the history of salvation when God intervened to bring life into hopeless situations. Here are three striking ones:

- *God gives Abraham's wife Sarah* a son when her age has made childbearing impossible. She laughs about it, and for this reason calls him Isaac. Later Abraham understood this so well and his faith in the promise was so firm that he was even ready to sacrifice this son. He believed that God was able to raise him from the dead.[27]
- *The virgin Mary* is a symbol of the hope of God's people who wait for salvation. In Luke 1:38 she recognises that God redeems lost humanity and that salvation comes from God alone, not from human action: 'Behold, the servant of the Lord; let it be done to me according to your word.' God enters the emptiness of life with its fears and crises, and

27. Hebrews 11:17-19.

gives His Son without any human means. According to the promise Jesus will save His people from their sins.

- *Mary Magdalene finds the tomb empty* on resurrection Sunday. When she meets Jesus, she confesses, 'My Lord and my God'. The living person of Jesus who came back from the dead is the epicentre of Christian hope for life beyond death and the new creation. He broke the power of cancelled sin, the power of death, and the power of Satan.

These three cases indicate that Christian hope points to eternity. It models hope in God in a hopeless world. The empty tomb negates all earthly hopes. We don't look there, but to the living Jesus. The grace of God reprograms our existence and His intervention creates new life and hope in the risen Christ.

A top-down perspective

As followers of Christ we bear fruit because our expectations and our mission in life are transformed by growing into Christ. The contrast between our unfruitful past, with its 'sterile works of darkness,' and the present, is stark, as underlined by key texts such as Ephesians 2.

Before becoming believers, we were living completely for ourselves; God was nothing at all. Even worse, we were hardly aware of our obsessions. Because our life has been renewed in Christ a big reset has taken place. God becomes our all in all, and our own interests are shifted from their pedestal. We become increasingly aware that living because of Him and in Him, we live for Him. Even more, present life is not the be-all and end-all. Every true Christian has something to look forward to and can say the best is yet to come!

How does this new perspective work out in our daily lives? The main thing is that because we are no longer enthralled by the world's agenda, we can take critical distance from what preoccupies those around us. Being in Christ implies having a different view from the current mentality, and developing a sceptical way of looking at what it takes to be the supreme good. We are no longer going to swallow what is served up. That's not difficult either, because what the world appreciates has lost its taste. So we are freed to stand back and let the rat race run its course.

To illustrate: a few years ago my wife and I went up the Rockefeller building in New York early one beautiful May morning. There were few people around and it was spectacular, looking down on the broad sweep of the 'Big Apple'. What a contrast to a few minutes earlier when down below on the street we had felt hemmed in and oppressed by towers of glass and concrete. Emerging at the top of the 'Rock' gave a totally different and beautiful outlook on the city.

Well, when we are in Christ we get elevated over the world's agendas and manias. As Lord of all Jesus Christ is above everything. He has the keys of life and death, in Him is all wisdom and knowledge, and we know He will return as promised to sort out this mess. A renewed mind looks at the world's problems from this critical perspective. Everything is different now from when we were hemmed in and slowly suffocated by the pressures of the world's ideologies. This is the life—to be our real selves free from posturing, and free to love not just some ideals, but our neighbours and even our enemies.[28] So as we press on to the higher calling of the Lord, we are confident that fruit will be borne to His glory. Three features characterise a view of life with this top-down perspective. These attitudes are conditions for bearing fruit in Christ.

28. Jesus' teaching in Luke 6:32-36 sets the bar much higher than anything prescribed by the ever-online social activists.

1. No future in progress

In a famous commencement address at the American University, Washington DC in June 1963, President John F. Kennedy affirmed his confidence in human progress:

> Our problems are man-made—therefore, they can be solved by man. And man can be as big as he wants. No problem of human destiny is beyond human beings. Man's reason and spirit have often solved the seemingly unsolvable—and we believe they can do it again.

The following November Kennedy was tragically assassinated in Dallas, Texas. His faith in man let him down. To this optimism a top-down biblical perspective will say *No!* Progress will not solve any of our problems, it will only aggravate them, as every human invention, from the wheel to artificial intelligence, illustrates. Nothing invented by man will deliver him from the inevitable destiny of sin and death. The writer of the book of Ecclesiastes learnt from experience that things do not get better. They may appear so, and none of us would want to return to the fourteenth century as a vacation destination. But life on earth is the same-old, same-old round of 'vanity of vanities, all is vanity'. In Christ we burst the bubble of human optimism, since He offers us a better and real hope.

2. The illusion of autonomy and neutrality

For over two centuries the West has lived with the myth of autonomy. This is based on the idea of neutrality. The modern mentality is that reality is not created, it has nothing to tell us about God, it is just there, or perhaps it's not there at all! We are free to make it what we want. Religion is just a subjective feeling to be excluded from the objective public sphere. As human beings become insensitive to nature as the work of

God's hands, proclaiming His glory, they end up either trying to dominate it, or worshipping it as our 'Mother'. This cult demands that they become the custodians protecting Mother's future from extinction. It's very short-sighted because natural forces show just how tiny humans are. Neutrality leads to autonomy and autonomy leads to the follies that flow from human self-promotion. As God's love is educated out of us, and our minds are mismanaged with great skill by autonomy and neutrality, destruction is programmed in.

The top-down perspective shows that the worship of God has a much surer outcome for humanity than if our future were to be left to the planning orgies of the Davos manipulators. The Master of the universe is the one who has already interpreted the meaning of His creation; our apprehension of it is only secondary. If we do not see creation in line with God's goodness in Christ we are mislead in our view of what it adds up to.

3. God's perspective

Looking at the world from a biblical perspective provides us with a new default setting for looking at life. The universe with its history bears the marks of a living and loving God, as well as the follies of man's sinful rejection of Him. Neutral ideas about life without God only make the universe into an impersonal wilderness where man takes over. This sums up the problem of the twentieth century and the disasters it brought. God have mercy!

Biblical revelation, on the other hand, shapes our world and life view so as to realign it with the reality of creation and a personal God. Believers in God *presuppose* that God and His intelligent plan is at the back of all things, visible and invisible. Everything bears the stamp of a landlord who is both sovereign and personal. The top-down perspective on life is based on the following fundamentals:

- God is independent: He exists eternally, before all things;[29]
- God is Triune: Father, Son and Holy Spirit are loving and personal;[30]
- God's intelligence is infinite: God has a plan for His creation;[31]
- God creates outside Himself: He gives meaning to every fact;[32]
- Created reality has the value that God gives it in the context of His plan;[33]
- God alone reveals God: He does so in creation, in Christ, and through His Word, the Holy Scriptures.[34]

Finally, this default position based on faith in God as true and the Bible as His revelation is nothing to be ashamed of. The alternative to biblical hope is a world that has no meaning where time and chance see us all off. Yet unbelievers live as though life had some meaning, which is highly contradictory.

A top-down perspective will bear fruit in believing lives since it has two takeaways—it frees us from the illusions that dominate the present, and opens our lives to freedom in Christ, to grow in Him in the perspective of eternity.

---

29. Exodus 3:14, Psalm 90:2.
30. John 3:35-36, 5:20.
31. John 1:1-3, Galatians 4:24.
32. Romans 11:33-36.
33. Ephesians 1:21-22.
34. Psalm 33.

Conclusion

Believers bear fruit in Christ by living in a self-consciously antithetical way to those around them. There is no middle way of compromise. We must learn to be critical dissenters, like the early Church and the first Protestants. This will no doubt set us apart from the aspirations and behaviour of our contemporaries, but that can't be a bad thing if we are fulfilling our calling to holiness in Christ, can it?

There are four pointers that may help evaluate whether we are bearing fruit in following Jesus:

- *Our motivation*: do we seek above all to glorify God?

Growth comes from progressive renewal in conformity to the mind of Christ.

- *Direction*: do we seek a deeper relationship with the living God?

Rather than looking out for ourselves, we make God our primary concern.

- *Perspective*: does God's Word set our direction?

This is the norm: what God approves, we love; what is opposed to His truth and His will is a lie; disobedience to God harms our spiritual welfare.

- *Clarity of mind*: do we exercise discernment?

The contrast between truth and error is crucial. What is 'Christian' is what lines up with biblical truth and promotes obedience to the Lord Jesus.

Given these conditions, fruit will grow to the glory of God.

QUESTIONS FOR DISCUSSION

1. Give an overview of the development of Christian growth to this point.
2. What does it mean to bear fruit?
3. Where is real fruit borne?
4. How is Christ the firstfruits?
5. How are we to glorify God?
6. What is the role of hope in bearing fruit?
7. What is the fruit of the Spirit and how does it differ from gifts?
8. What can hold us back from bearing fruit?
9. What is a top-down view of the world?
10. Discuss ways you could grow better into Christ.

CONCLUSION

LESSONS IN ENCOURAGEMENT

Discouragement and encouragement
Caring for others
Rising to the challenge
Serving others in Christ
Bearing the burden with others

Conclusion theme: *Spiritual growth in Christ is stimulated by encouragement. It takes the needs of others to heart by caring for them, accepting their challenges with them, and serving by bearing their burdens with them. Barnabas in the Acts of the Apostles is a model of how encouragement leads to growth in Christ's service.*

One of the contributing factors to growth in Christ is encouragement. In 1 Thessalonians 5:11 Paul exhorts believers to 'encourage one another and build one another up, just as you are doing.' We grow in grace when we are encouraged by the help and example of others, by God's Word, by prayer, and by biblical teaching. To grow we need all the encouragement we can get from the right sources.

Discouragement hampers development, including in the spiritual realm. It attacks from the outside and puts a brake on growth in Christ. It may arise from a criticism, an accident, an unexpected setback, or from the realisation of the problems our sin has caused. Most of us are easily deflated, withdraw into ourselves, and this cuts us off from Christ and the source of life in Him. Fortunately, the psychological push-back of discouragement doesn't always correspond to the real situation. The causes or consequences of discouragement may be more imagined than real. We become our own worst enemies by self-pitying introspection.

Continual discouragement often leads to depression and fatigue. We disengage by sidelining ourselves and in the end we despair and are burned out. Perhaps we engage in passive aggressive behaviour to those around us, and discouragement makes us want to give up. There's a bit of that in the disciples reply to Jesus in Luke 5:5: 'we have toiled all night and took nothing!' However, eter knew better than to quit: 'at your word I will let down the nets'. He found encouragement in the presence of Jesus, and gave it another go, with unexpected results.

Encouragement comes via support from someone or some unexpected circumstance. It may take a lot to encourage us. However, contrary to its opposite, encouragement is more often than not rooted in reality, and it tends to be objective, not imaginary. Our brothers and sisters are invariably our best allies and their encouragement supports us and raises hope; it perks us up, sets the adrenaline working and leads to renewed involvements.

If little good comes from discouragement, which gathers speed like a helter-skelter, encouragement is an upward spiral and leads to greater encouragements and attainments. It's obvious that the church should be a place of encouragement.[1] However, it's much easier to discourage others than it is to encourage, either in ministry or as members of the congregation. Often we are not aware of how discouraging and negative our attitudes are. Because of that it's useful to look at a concrete case of encouragement in Scripture and see what it involves.

Caring for others' welfare

In Acts 4:36-37 we meet up with one Joseph, a Levite (an assistant of the priests) who hailed from Cyprus. The apostles gave him the nickname Barnabas meaning son of encouragement, because he was that by name and by nature. Without his contribution to the growth of the early Church, there might not have been an apostle Paul as we know him, and Christians might not have been called by that name. What Barnabas did initially was a small thing—selling a field and giving the proceeds to the apostles, in contrast with the cheating of Ananias and Saphira in the following chapter.

That sale marked the start of an exemplary life of encouragement contributing to growth in the Church. Barnabas was so-called because he was recognised as someone who acted positively in response to needs. His encouragement was appreciated by the apostles. He gave his substance for others and was obviously a person who thought of others at his own

1. 1 Thessalonians 5:11.

cost. He gave generously, honestly, without strings attached, and spontaneously.

So Barnabas' heart was laid bare in his altruistic action. He was an encourager in how he thought of others and their needs and was touched by their difficulties. Encouragement involves sensitivity and discernment, followed by sincere and appropriate action.

Rising to the challenge

We run into Barnabas again later, in Acts 9:26-27, at a crucial moment. The newly converted Saul was an enigmatic outsider to believers, a *persona non grata*, suspected by Christians and Jews alike. Is he a traitor, or is he a spy? Barnabas has faith and is open-minded enough to believe that God can do what humanly seems impossible. By taking Saul under his wing he became involved in a situation where he could have lost face. It worked. Having Barnabas beside him encouraged Saul and opened the way for his recognition by the Church. Barnabas was willing to break with the mistrust that leads to discouragement and so counter the native fear of those around him. This was the love of Jesus at work since, as 1 John 4:18 states, 'perfect love casts out fear'. Barnabas accepted the challenge, got alongside Saul, supported him by becoming his advocate, convinced of what the Lord had done in Saul's life. Barnabas' faith in God, and his clear-mindedness about what the Lord can do, overcame reticence and suspicion. His spiritual discernment enabled him to take on the challenge of being Saul's supporter. This was a crucial moment, not only for Saul, but also in the growth of the early Church.

Serving others in Christ

Barnabas' next outing as an encourager happened when the church in Jerusalem sent him to Antioch because of the many people there who had believed in the gospel. In Acts 11:22-30 we have a sketch of his activity in around 43 A.D. In Antioch he 'saw the grace of God, was glad, and exhorted them to remain faithful to the Lord with steadfast purpose, for he was a good man, full of the Holy Spirit and of faith'. The result of his action was that even more people were 'added to the Lord'. So what did Barnabas do then? He sought out Saul, over in Tarsus in Asia Minor (about 150 miles away) and brought him back to Antioch, where they stayed together for a year and a 'great many people' were discipled. Subsequently when Agabus and some prophets came down from Jerusalem, the Antioch church was forewarned of the famine in Jerusalem, and sent relief by Barnabas and Saul.

What a picture of Barnabas is presented in a few verses! He was a person of vision, a good and caring worker, 'full of the Holy Spirit' and of 'faith', that is practical trust in the Lord. His spiritual qualities allowed him to appreciate in Saul (soon to become Paul the apostle), the value of someone who would do a great job. Furthermore he was prepared to make way for Paul's qualities. He encouraged him and so Paul grew into the apostle he would become.

Bearing the burden with others

Acts 13 and 14 recount Paul's first missionary journey as an apostle.[2] Up to that point Barnabas and Saul are spoken of, but now the order changes to Paul and Barnabas. Barnabas was like the cyclist who sets up the sprint for the team leader and then

2. Acts 13:7, 43, 46, 50, Acts 14:12, 14, 20.

pulls aside to let him win. Barnabas carries the burden with his fellow worker and shows the sterling character of someone who knows how to encourage others:

- He is alongside Paul in the difficulties and the joys of ministry—a stalwart who sticks at it when trials befall. The rejection of Paul's message finds a sympathiser in Barnabas (13:50, 14:20);
- With Paul he perseveres in the work (14:21-27) even when the going is tough. They 'strengthen the souls of the disciples, encouraging them to continue in the faith and saying that "through many tribulations we must enter the kingdom of God".'

The remarkable thing about Barnabas is that he knows the value of being a good no.2, and he accepts that not everyone is called to be a no.1. He's the model of those believers who work humbly with a spirit of self-effacement.

Encouragement implies being altruistic, because ultimately the Lord's cause is more important than our causes. This is also the model of Jesus who humbled Himself, submitting to the will of His Father to do His work.[3]

Encouragement and growth is in Christ

The beautiful story of the joint ministry of Paul and Barnabas ends, after the Jerusalem council in Acts 15, with disillusionment and disagreement.[4] This in itself reminds us of something important. Although very impactful and important, human encouragement is limited in time and usefulness. The real 'encourager' is the Lord Himself; His servants are only

3. Phillipians 2:8.
4. Acts 15:2, 12, 22, 25, 35-39.

instruments and their encouragement is always secondary. Growth is 'in Christ' and encouragement is a means to that end. The disagreement between Paul and Barnabas is not a doctrinal but a personal one. Doctrinal differences are often insoluble, because they involve truth questions, whereas personal disagreements find reconciliation. In 1 Corinthians 9:6 Paul refers to Barnabas indicating that they had been reconciled and had renewed communion one with another.

So others may let us down and fail us, and we also fall short of our own expectations. However, the Lord's encouragement knows no such limitations. Ultimately it's His promises and grace that encourage us.[5] This teaches us to relativize and not to exaggerate times of disagreement or failure. They are like tunnels through which the Lord leads us through darkness to a greater appreciation of divine wisdom and providence in the growth of His people. Failures are necessary and keep us dependent, not on men, but on God and His grace.

Encouraging one another

The model of Barnabas illustrates that the encouragement of others promotes their spiritual growth and the development of the Church of Christ.

An encouraging attitude is not a question of personality but a spiritual gift, a capacity to be developed, a challenge, and a form of service that puts others before ourselves. Being an encourager involves making oneself available to support others, to listen, and to understand them. It implies accepting danger or inconvenience by carrying others' burdens, sometimes getting involved in trial and hardship in a way we would rather avoid.

---

5. Note the way Jesus restored Peter after he had denied his master, John 21:15-19.

Finally, if encouragement comes via others, it ultimately flows from the Lord Jesus and His Word. As Hebrews 10:24-25 exhorts: 'Let us consider how to stir up one another to love and good works, not neglecting to meet together, as is the habit of some, but encouraging one another, and all the more as you see the Day drawing near.' Such words give us the assurance that despite difficult times, trials, and even persecution, nothing will prevent a believer's growth into Christ, or separate them from the love of God in Him.

QUESTIONS FOR DISCUSSION

1. What is discouraging you at present?
2. What steps can you take to turn this situation around?
3. How do others in the church discourage you?
4. What can you do about it?
5. How can you become an encouragement to others?
6. How does Barnabas encourage you to become a support for those around you?
7. Who are the people you should be helping?
8. What can you do to encourage the leaders of your church community?
9. How can you support those around you, spouse, children, parents, neighbours?
10. How do you find encouragement in the person of Christ?

APPENDIX

Reading the Bible and praying are essential to growth in Christ. But it's not always obvious how to go about it...

Here are some suggestions that can be adapted to your personal needs.

Reading the Bible-personal method

1. First, ask the Lord to help you focus your thoughts.
2. Read the Scripture, one or more chapters, aloud if possible, and then select a short text.
3. Write this text in a notebook (or on your phone) and memorise it.

4. Meditate on the meaning of your reading and apply it to your life situation. For instance what does 'taste and see that the Lord is good' (Psalm 34:8) mean for you?
5. Repeat its meaning for yourself, so as to stimulate your affections for God and His grace.
6. Decide what you will do (a particular action or change of attitude) as a result.
7. Sing a hymn and pray again to dedicate yourself to the Lord's service.

Prayer-personal method

1. Follow the order of Jesus' prayer in Matthew 6:9-13—first God and then our needs.
2. Call on God as your Father, through the mediation of the Son, and seek the Holy Spirit's assistance.
3. Praise God by repeating what you have read in His Word.
4. Observe in the course of your prayer:
    - Praise God for who He is (His attributes)
    - Confess your sins and failures
    - Seek help for your needs and fears (the day and the week)
    - Thank Him for what He has given you (His grace)
    - Dedicate yourself to His service (small beginnings are important).
5. Extend your prayer to others (the importance of the fruits of the Spirit). Make a prayer list for:
    - your family and friends

- your church and its leaders. (For example, pray for a member of your leadership team each day)
- the mission of the Church in the world, and persecuted believers
- your country and its elected representatives.[1]

6. Read and sing psalms and hymns to the glory of God.

1. For instance for persecuted Christians, Open doors, https://media.opendoorsuk.org/document/pdf/Prayer%20Diary.pdf. For this country, the Christian Institute, https://www.christian.org.uk.

100 Devotional Readings
on Union With Christ
HOW TO LIVE AN
'IN CHRIST' LIFE
KENNETH BERDING

How to Live an 'In Christ' Life

100 Devotional Readings on Union with Christ

Kenneth Berding

- 'In Christ' phrases from New Testament
- Identity, life, community and mission
- 100 devotions

Everywhere we look in the letters of Paul we encounter 'in Christ.' But how many of us know why the Apostle Paul uses this expression—or ones like it—over and over again in his letters? What is so important about being in Christ? Is it possible that when Paul talks about *inChristness*, he is handing us a set of keys that will open up his letters and reveal what is most essential to living the Christian life? In these 100 devotional readings, we discover why *inChristness* is so important and how to live an in–Christ life.

ISBN: 978-1-5271-0559-1

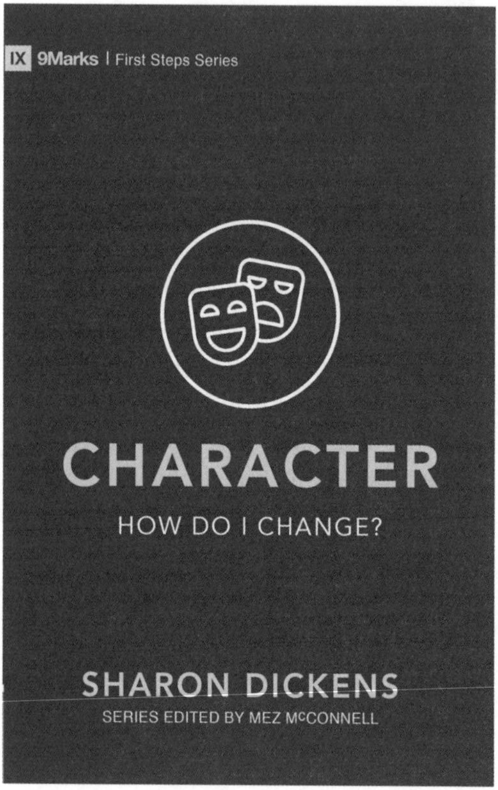
IX 9Marks | First Steps Series
CHARACTER
HOW DO I CHANGE?
SHARON DICKENS
SERIES EDITED BY MEZ McCONNELL

Character

How Do I Change?

Sharon Dickens

- Part of the First Steps series
- For new Christians
- How to grow in godliness

So, you've heard the Gospel, you've accepted Jesus as your saviour, you're going to Church regularly – you're definitely a Christian, but you don't feel like you're acting like one. The other Christians you know all seem to have it together but how do you get to that point? Even though none of us will be perfect in this life, we can grow to be more and more like Jesus. This book will tell you how.

ISBN: 978-1-5271-0101-2

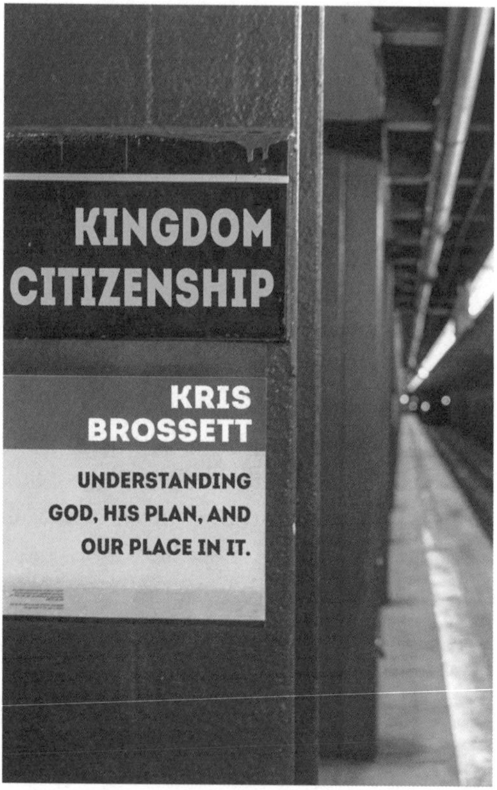
KINGDOM CITIZENSHIP
KRIS BROSSETT
UNDERSTANDING GOD, HIS PLAN, AND OUR PLACE IN IT.

Kingdom Citizenship

Understanding God, His Plan, and Our Place in it

Kris Brossett

- 6–Week Study
- Brokenness, Promise, Grace, Sanctification, Church & Christian Walk

Everyone grows up, but maturity is a choice. In the same way, becoming a mature Christian requires a choice to actively pursue spiritual growth. It's important to learn what the Bible teaches about God and to obey what you learn. Whether you're a new Christian, you've been a Christian for a long time, or you're interested in Christianity, this six–week study will help you to know God, to live boldly for Him, and to grow into Christian maturity.

ISBN: 978-1-5271-0410-5

EVERYDAY

HOLINESS

Becoming Who You Were Made to Be

Josh Moody

Everyday Holiness

Becoming Who You Were Made to Be

Josh Moody

Dr. Josh Moody leads us with clarity along a path to a simple biblical profundity: holiness is becoming who we are in Christ. Holiness isn't about a drab or dreary lifestyle. It's not about faking it, or being inauthentic. Holiness is becoming who you were made to be. There's a sweetness, a joy, a freedom in pursuing Jesus. We were designed to live like this, so we find our fullest flourishing there.

ISBN: 978-1-5271-0725-0

God's Spirit

The Antidote to Chaos

Reuben Hunter

God's Spirit

The Antidote to Chaos

Reuben Hunter

To live well in this world, we need more than to just try harder. If we want lives that are marked by love, joy and peace, if we want to see goodness planted in the soil of our marriages and families, we need something we can't actually drum up from inside ourselves, however hard we try or how disciplined we become. The truth is, we need someone to come from outside of us to empower us to live the good life. The good life not on my terms but on God's terms. It is His world, and He wants us to live a certain way. But He doesn't just say try harder, He comes to us in the person of His Spirit, to enable us to grow into those people, to more closely resemble His Son, the Lord Jesus.

ISBN: 978-1-5271-0839-4

Christian Focus Publications

Our mission statement –

STAYING FAITHFUL
In dependence upon God we seek to impact the world through literature faithful to His infallible Word, the Bible. Our aim is to ensure that the Lord Jesus Christ is presented as the only hope to obtain forgiveness of sin, live a useful life and look forward to heaven with Him.

Our Books are published in four imprints:

CHRISTIAN FOCUS

popular works including biographies, commentaries, basic doctrine and Christian living.

CHRISTIAN HERITAGE

books representing some of the best material from the rich heritage of the church.

MENTOR

books written at a level suitable for Bible College and seminary students, pastors, and other serious readers. The imprint includes commentaries, doctrinal studies, examination of current issues and church history.

CF4•K

children's books for quality Bible teaching and for all age groups: Sunday school curriculum, puzzle and activity books; personal and family devotional titles, biographies and inspirational stories – Because you are never too young to know Jesus!

Christian Focus Publications Ltd,
Geanies House, Fearn, Ross-shire,
IV20 1TW, Scotland, United Kingdom.
www.christianfocus.com